The Military in the Middle East

Problems in Society and Government

The Graduate Institute for World Affairs, No. 1

A Publication of the Mershon Center for Education in National Security

Ohio State University Press ● Columbus 1963

The Military in the Middle East

Problems in Society and Government ● **Edited by Sydney Nettleton Fisher**

Preface

THE PAPERS contained in this volume were presented at the Graduate Institute for World Affairs of the Ohio State University during a three-day conference, November 30—December 2, 1961, on the subject "The Role of the Military in Society and Government in the Middle East." It was an open gathering with formal papers, invited discussion leaders for each paper, and free and informal discussion concluding each session.

Dr. John C. Campbell had the difficult assignment of drawing together the points of the several papers and the comments and valuable contributions of the ensuing discussions. His synthesis was so well received by the conference that many suggested that his remarks and pertinent observations, rather than be lost, should be included in the published proceedings of the conference. He was persuaded to compose his thoughts and conclusions into an article, and, thus, his essay should be read in this light.

In conjunction with this conference, Dr. William R. Polk gave an address as the inaugural ceremony for the opening of the Graduate Institute for World Affairs. Since the timeliness and significance of his words coincided in part with the topic of this conference, it has been considered suitable to include his address as an appendix to this volume.

Each contributor has revised his paper benefiting from more hindsight, the generous advice and counsel of those in attendance, and the observations and suggestions of numerous other friends and colleagues. Editing has been kept at the barest minimum.

The authors of the several papers wish to indicate here their indebtedness to the following persons in attendance at the conference for the range and relevance of their private and public comments: Dr. Mohamed el-Behairy, Defiance College; Major Shepherd A. Booth, Department of the Army; Professor Wen-yu Cheng, Marietta College; Professor C. Ernest Dawn, University of Illinois; Colonel Donald J. Decker, National War College; Mr. John Devlin, Washington, D.C.; Professor Gifford B. Doxsee, Ohio University; Dr. Martin E. Dulgarian, Miami University (Ohio); Mr. Nuri Eren, Princeton University; Mr. Francis G. Erlenwein, Fort Hayes; Ambassador Waldemar J. Gallman, Washington, D.C.; Dr. David E. Gardinier, Bowling Green State University; Mr. James Q. Graham, Bowling Green State University; Mr. Foster Hailey, *New York Times;* Miss Jeanne Haskett, Central Michigan University; Father Johnson, Xavier University; Captain Thomas D. Keegan, Ohio State University; Captain Russell Kefauver, Department of the Navy; Colonel Michael K. Kettlehut, Department of State; Professor Ch'ung tai Lu, Baldwin-Wallace College; General S. L. A. Marshall, *Detroit News;* Commander Thomas L. Neilson, Department of the Navy; Major Henry A. Norman, Fort Hayes; Colonel John S. Patton, Department of the Air Force; Professor Richard H. Pfaff, University of Colorado; Professor John R. Randall, Ohio State University; Colonel Donald G. Renwick, Ohio State University; Professor William Schorger, University of Michigan; Dr. Richard F. S. Starr, Washington, D.C.; Professor Harold Stein, Prineston University and the University of Michigan; General Samuel G. Taxis, Department of Defense; Professor Peter Topping, University of Cincinnati; Captain Charles R. Wallis, United States Military Academy; Dean Everett Walters, Ohio State University; Colonel Gordon G. Warner, Ohio State University; Colonel E. R. White, Joint Chiefs of Staff; and President Herrick Young, Western College for Women.

SYDNEY NETTLETON FISHER

Contents

The Military in the Middle East

Problems in Society and Government

The Military in Middle Eastern Society and Politics DANKWART A. RUSTOW

THERE are few major regions of the world where the military have played as prominent or profound a political role as in the Middle East. No international wars have been fought in the Middle East since the end of World War II, except for the Palestine War of 1948-49 and the abortive Sinai-Suez campaign of 1956. Yet the intervention of the armed forces and their officers in the domestic political process has been frequent, drastic, and profound.[1] The Egyptian revolution of 1952 replaced King Faruq and the Wafd party with a military regime. Two years later, General Nagib was ousted by Colonel Nasir. In 1958, Syria joined Egypt in the United Arab Republic after a prolonged crisis in which the army played a leading role; and in September, 1961, as a result of another military revolt, Syria dissolved the three-year-old union. In Iran, the Shah was restored to his throne in 1953 by action of the armed forces under General Zahidi. The year 1958 set an all-time record for political intervention by the military: the Iraqi revolution installed the regime of General Qasim; in Lebanon, a brief civil war was terminated by the intervention of U. S. marines and the inauguration of General Shihab as President of the Republic; in Jordan, the Arab Legion, with a brief assist from British forces, secured the con-

3

tinued rule of King Husayn; and the army in Pakistan, under General Ayub, and in the Sudan, under General Abbud, displayed parliamentary government. Finally, in May, 1960, the Turkish armed forces termin- ated the oppressive regime of Premier Menderes, making way a year later for a second parliamentary republic headed by ex-General Gürsel as President and ex-General Inönü as Prime Minister. All in all, at the beginning of 1962, nine of the thirteen countries of the region had political regimes installed or dominated by the armed forces and their officer corps.

Before turning, in the chapters that follow, to a more detailed examination of the contemporary role of the military in individual countries, it will be appropriate to take a comprehensive look at the region as a whole and at the historical, cultural, and social factors that have propelled the military so dramatically and ubiquitously upon the Middle Eastern political scene.

CLUBS ARE TRUMPS

Politics, Thomas Hobbes once suggested, is like a game of cards: the players must agree which card is to be trump. With this difference, he adds, that in politics, whenever no other card is agreed upon, clubs are trumps.[2] Here is one important explanation of the army's role in Middle Eastern politics and one to which there will be occasion to return in later contexts. Lack of agreement on basic constitutional principles, inexperience with government by discussion, weakness of civilian bureaucracies, atrophy of political parties, and diffuseness of economic interest groups—all of these contribute to an atmosphere where violence becomes not only the ultima ratio, but all too often the prima ratio of politics. It is no coincidence that the four countries of the area which have had no military coups or revolutions in the last decade lie at the two extremes, tradition and modernity, of the cultural spectrum. They include the three remaining patriarchal monarchies of the region— Yemen, Afghanistan, and Saudi Arabia—where petroleum and com- petitive foreign aid have only just begun to revolutionize agricultural or nomadic subsistence economies. And they include Israel, where the population, composed at first largely of European immigrants, has created a parliamentary system of government based on tightly organ-

4

ized, pluralistic parties and interest groups. It is in the middle ranges of the spectrum that the military become a factor to reckon with—in countries caught in the profound and unsettling process of transition from traditional Islam to modern secularism, from feudal or subsistence agriculture to urbanism and industry, from an ascriptive class structure to social mobility, from semi-colonial rule toward national self-government.

Yet, even in this middle spectrum, Hobbes' aphorism explains only part of the story. The military in the Middle East not only fill the contemporary vacuum left by lack of agreement on the political rules of the game; there are also positive historical factors to account for their prominence. Or, to use a simile recently popularized by Gamal Abd al-Nasir, the military not only have responded to the challenge of a political "role in search of a hero,"[3] they have also played an important historical role (if perhaps not always a heroic one) in their own right.

ISLAMIC AND OTTOMAN ANTECEDENTS

Because of its focal geographic position at the juncture of three continents and two oceans, the Middle East has been, throughout recorded history, the most frequently invaded region of the globe. Alexander of Macedon and Pompey of Rome came from the west, the early Islamic armies from the Arabian peninsula, Hulagu the Mongol and Timur the Turk from the north, and the Ottomans from Anatolia. More recently, the French, since the days of Napoleon, and the British, since the days of Nelson and Kitchener, have vied for power in the region; and since the end of World War II, the Middle East has become the stage for conflicting Russian and American military interests.

Out of the kaleidoscopic array of conquests and invasions, three forces may be singled out whose historical influence is felt to this day: the advent of Islam, the rise and fall of the Ottoman Empire, and the impact of the modern West.

Islam arose in the seventh century A.D. as a conquering faith which unified, within a century after the Prophet's death, a vast region from the Pyrenees to the Pamirs and imposed on most of it a religious and cultural stamp which thirteen centuries have not deleted. Compared with other world religions, Islam in its theology and jurisprudence accords a high degree of legitimacy to warfare. The doctrine of *jihad*, or Holy War, for example, asserts that the true faith can be spread by conquest as well as by conversion; Muslim international law rests on a basic distinction between the Abode of War and the Abode of Islam; *amir al-mu'minin*, or Commander of the Faithful, is one of the most frequently used titles of the Caliph . . .

and Muslim political philosophers have generally held effective exercise of power to be the chief or sole criterion of governmental legitimacy.

Within the early Islamic domain, the Ottoman state . . . emerged as one of the many principalities founded by frontier warriors along the northern marches. The Ottoman victory over Byzantium (1453) initiated a century of spectacular conquest which carried Ottoman rule as far as Algeria, Hungary, the Ukraine, Iraq, and Yemen. Throughout Ottoman history the army, along with the Sultan's palace establishment, remained the largest, most elaborate, and most expensive part of the Empire's "ruling institution"; and the decline of Ottoman military fortunes in the protracted contest with the Habsburg and Romanov Empires only served to reinforce the military's central position. The impact of modern Europe on the Ottoman Empire was felt most acutely as a military impact—from the breaking of the second siege of Vienna (1683) to Bonaparte's invasion of Egypt (1798) and down to the Great War of 1914-1918. The Ottomans' natural reaction was to try to borrow, first and foremost, the "cutting edge" of Western civilization. With the importation of European military instructors, which began in the late eighteenth century, and the substitution of a newly organized army for the dissolute Janissary corps (1826), the army officers became one of the most Westernized elements in the Empire. The officers corps had always had a wide base of social and geographic recruitment; as a result of the nineteenth-century reforms, it also became one of the most conspicuous channels for merit advancement within the Empire's social structure.[4]

The Ottoman Empire during the reign of Mahmud II and in the days of the *Tanzimat,* and Egypt under Muhammad Ali and his successors, provide two classic illustrations of European military threats as a stimulus for cultural change and of the armed forces as the spearhead of modernization in politics, economics, and society. In both countries administrative and fiscal systems were overhauled to pay for the more expensive modernized army; public works were undertaken to accommodate its strategic requirements; industry fostered to serve its needs of procurement; and higher education instituted to fill its command positions. Mathematics and science, medicine and European languages were introduced first into the military curriculum and only later in separate civilian schools.

Within the rising westernized elite, military cadets and officers were

6

among the first converts to liberal European ideas of constitutionalism and nationalism. In 1881, Egyptian officers under Colonel 'Urābi attempted the first modern military coup in the Middle East, aimed primarily at subjecting the spendthrift Khedive to the financial control of a representative assembly. A few years later, students at the Ottoman army medical college founded the Society of Union and Progress—the nucleus of the conspiracy which, in the 1908 revolution, overthrew the despotism of Sultan Abdülhamid. The facile tendency of the triumphant Union and Progress officers to equate Ottomanism with Turkish nationalism led to the formation of secret societies among Ottoman Arab officers, who in turn became the first nationalist leaders in the countries of the Fertile Crescent. After the Ottoman defeat of 1918, the ranking generals on active duty, such as Mustafa Kemal [Atatürk], Kâzim Karabekir, and Ali Fuad [Cebesoy], co-operated with local civilian leaders in organizing the Defense of Rights movement in Anatolia, which won the Turkish War of Independence and created the Republican People's party and the First Turkish Republic.

WESTERN IMPACT

The modernization program of the nineteenth century and the role of army officers in nationalist movements of the twentieth were part of the Middle Eastern response to European military expansionism. But the imperialist challenge itself set important precedents for the crucial role of military action in contemporary Middle Eastern politics. The 'Urābi revolt led, in 1882, to the so-called temporary occupation of Egypt by British forces—an occupation which, in one form or another, was to last fully seventy-four years. Throughout this period, British intervention in Egyptian politics was backed repeatedly by military action or military threat—most notably in 1919, 1924, and 1942. In the Fertile Crescent, British and French mandates were established in the wake of World War I. But the benevolent educational theories of the mandates were quickly belied by the coercive measures required to instal and maintain the new regimes. In Damascus, where Faysal had been proclaimed King of Greater Syria in 1919, French troops surrounded and occupied the city despite Faysal's acceptance of their peremptory ultimatum. The revolt of the nomadic tribes in the

7

Middle Euphrates region of Iraq, in 1921, and in the Druze Mountains of Syria, in 1925, prompted massive military action by the British and the French. In Transjordan the British set up a client government, whose mainstays were an annual subsidy from the British treasury and the British-officered, bedouin-recruited Arab Legion. In Palestine the mandatory government's self-contradictory policy exacerbated the sharp contrast between Arab and Jewish aspirations and at length resulted in a three-cornered civil war.

In World War II, the Middle East was not involved in any of the military operations, except along the Libyan front. Yet the area's pivotal strategic location prompted the Allies to take no chances on an interruption of their lines of communication or on a gradual drift of individual countries into the Axis camp. Again and again, military intervention to change domestic political regimes was the last resort: in the spring of 1941, the suppression of the pro-Axis Rashid Ali government in Iraq by British and Transjordanian forces; a few weeks later, the ejection of Vichy forces from Syria and Lebanon by British and De Gaullist troops; that same summer, the unceremonious occupation of Iran by British and Russian contingents, followed by the deposition and exile of Shah Riza; and early in 1942, British tanks surrounding King Faruq's palace in Cairo to force replacement of a pro-Italian with a pro-British cabinet.

Not only was Western power throughout the Middle East installed and maintained by force, but the relinquishment of these same power positions came generally in response to the assertion of equal or superior force. The Egyptian nationalist uprising of 1919 brought to the scene the Milner commission, which recommended, for the first time, direct dealings with the exiled nationalist leaders. The precarious reassertion of British control over Iraq in 1941 was followed at once by a shift of British policy toward cautious support of Pan-Arab aspirations. In 1945-46, it took the threat of British military intervention to force French evacuation from Syria in pursuance of a joint Anglo-French wartime undertaking. And in 1956, blunt warnings from the United States—as well as from the Soviet Union—forced the abandonment of the concerted Israeli-French-British attack on Egypt.

This is not to deny that some of the Western policies just reviewed, particularly those during World War II, may have been amply justified

8

by overriding moral considerations. Still the fact remains that the Middle East's experience with Western imperialism has greatly reinforced indigenous tendencies toward coercive politics. Looking at the situation from their viewpoint, one can hardly blame Middle Eastern leaders for suspecting that Western doctrines of self-determination and constitutionalism were intended for domestic consumption and for concluding that, in the Middle East at least, military force alone could be counted upon for decisive results.

What, then, in brief is the legacy of Middle Eastern history as it bears on the present role of the military in society and politics? The Middle East, more than any comparable world region, has been subject to military invasions throughout history. Most states of the region, down to the present, have been established by conquest; most of the recent changes of regime have been effected by military action. The region's traditional culture rests upon a religion that accords great prestige and legitimacy to the military. And the direct and indirect impact of modernity upon the traditional culture further tended to enhance the leading role of the armed forces and their officer corps. Against this background, it is clear that the prominent and decisive role of the military on the current Middle Eastern scene is not a momentary lapse from normal constitutional practice but conforms to ample historical precedent. Conversely, it is the occasional spells of peaceful constitutional government by civilians—as in Turkey from 1922 to 1960, in Lebanon from 1945 to 1958, in Israel since 1948—which must be seen as the exceptional situations.

THE COMMON PATTERN OF MIDDLE EASTERN COUPS

The preceding historical survey has provided the necessary background for an examination of the more immediate circumstances in which Middle Eastern armies have wrested power from civilian governments or forced the replacement of one civilian government by another. Although the experiences of each country and each individual military coup offer a great many variations of detail, there are indeed some strikingly common features and patterns. Leaving a fuller analysis of individual cases for later chapters, these similarities can be summed

9

up under several headings and some hypotheses suggested to account for them.

There is a remarkable parallel in the timing of the initial military coups in Iraq, Syria, and Egypt. Iraq was released from mandate status in 1932; in 1936, General Bakr Sidqi performed his military coup, which, in the next five years, was to be followed by six others. In Syria, French occupation was withdrawn in mid-1945; in 1949, there were three successive military coups under Colonels Za'im, Hinnawi and Shishakli. In 1947, the British discontinued their wartime occupation of Egypt proper, concentrating their remaining troops in the Canal Zone; in 1952, the Free Officers seized power under General Nagib and Colonel Nasir. It is obvious that a military seizure of power by indigenous officers will not occur during foreign occupation; a colonial regime may expect army mutinies, as in India in 1857, but not coups d'état. The Middle Eastern evidence would seem to suggest that it takes four to five years after de facto independence for civilian institutions to be sufficiently discredited and the army officers sufficiently self-confident to set the stage for the first coup.

Armies commonly seize power on the domestic scene after defeat on the battlefield, not after victory. On this point, it may be argued that the historical evidence offers too few examples to support firm generalizations; but it is surely no coincidence that Turkish victory in the War of Independence of 1919-22 was followed by thirty-eight years of military subordination to orderly civilian rule, or that Israel, the one Middle Eastern country to win any battlefield victories in recent decades, is also the only country that has not had a single military coup. Instances on the converse side are equally striking: the Ottoman Empire's defeat in the First Balkan War was followed by the so-called Sublime Porte Incident of January, 1913, in which Enver, at the head of a gang of trigger-happy lieutenants, stormed the government offices in Istanbul, shot the war minister, forced the aging Grand Vezir Kâmil Pasha to write out his resignation at pistol point, and established the dictatorship of the famous Young Turk triumvirate of Enver, Cemal, and Talât. In 1919, the defeated Ottoman army under Mustafa Kemal organized nationalist resistance in Anatolia in open defiance of the Sultan and his collaborationist ministers. Finally, the Syrian coups of 1949 and the

10

Egyptian revolution of 1952 were in large part a response to the humiliation of defeat in the Palestine War.

Several convergent explanations may be suggested. The most disciplined and professionalized armies are likely to make the best showing in wartime and are also the likeliest to submit to civilian control. On the other hand, an army that is too weak to beat a foreign enemy still has ample strength to cow its unarmed domestic antagonists. Defeat in war, moreover, is likely to undermine popular confiidence in the existing government. The army itself—partly as a result of the psychological law that links frustration to aggression—is tempted to clear its tarnished record by finding a civilian scapegoat. Thus, Enver and his associates reproached Kâmil Pasha with lack of determination to recapture the former capital of Edirne; and Gamal Abd al-Nasir and his fellow conspirators blamed their defeat in Palestine on the inferior equipment supplied by Faruq's corrupt entourage. (It should be noted in passing that the Kemalist revolution does not fully fit this pattern, for here the target of military action was not, primarily, the Sultan but rather the invading Greek, Armenian, and French forces.)

Military coups follow upon a period of internal unrest in which civilian authorities have come increasingly to rely on armed forces to maintain themselves in power. On this point examples abound: The formative experience of the Young Turk conspirators of 1908 was the running and losing fight which Abdülhamid's government was carrying on against rebellious Christian elements in the Balkans and against defiant Arab vassals, such as the Imam of Yemen. Riza Khan, before his 1921 coup in Iran, had distinguished himself by suppressing the secessionist Gilan Soviet Republic. General Bakr Sidqi became a popular hero by his ruthless suppression of the Assyrian uprising in 1933 before seizing power in Baghdad three years later. The Egyptian revolution of 1952 was preceded by four years of near civil war. And the military revolutions in Iraq in 1958 and in Turkey in 1960 were preceded by several years of forcible suppression of political opposition; the Turkish upheaval, in particular, reflected the army's refusal to let itself be used any further as a tool of Menderes' repressive policies. In short, military seizure of power comes not as a sudden isolated departure but, more commonly, as the climax of a continuously growing military involvement upon the domestic scene—an involvement that adds

11

to the army's skills in domestic coercion and which makes the civilian government more dependent on the army and hence a more vulnerable and tempting target once the army decides on its *volte-face*. Where survival of a civilian government depends on armed power, a coup in which the army switches sides must, *ex hypothesi*, succeed. Prolonged defeat in internal war, as in the Ottoman Empire before 1908 (or in French Algeria in the 1950's), will heighten the army's frustration and hence speed its revolt.

Armed coups d'état occur when mounting popular dissatisfaction can find no peaceful means of forcing a change in government. This is in part a restatement of the previous theorem. It is also the situation that best fits Hobbes' dictum about clubs being trumps in politics whenever no other card is agreed upon. It is not entirely accurate to think of the army as filling a vacuum; rather it moves in to break a stalemate. An army coup, to succeed, needs civilian support, and the civilians will not lend such support until simpler and less risky avenues have been blocked. Hence the military coup is the standard antidote to traditional despotisms and modern dictatorships—including dictatorships established by previous military coups—as well as to entrenched oligarchies which have thwarted the parliamentary and electoral procedures prescribed in the constitutions.

The precise form of military-civilian co-operation varies. There may be a formal alliance, initiated by either side, between the military and civilian conspirators—as within the Ottoman Union and Progress Society in 1908-1913, between Riza Khan and Ziaeddin Tabatabai in Iran in 1921, or between Bakr Sidqi and the Iraqi Ikha party in 1936. There may be a looser ideological or organizational connection as between the Egyptian Officers and the Muslim Brethren in 1952. Or officers may act without any prior understanding but with confident assurance that their action will be welcomed by important segments of the public —such as the universities and the Republican People's party in Turkey in 1960.

There is an equally wide variety of actual techniques for a coup d'état—and it would be interesting to correlate these with the typology that abundant evidence has suggested to Latin American observers. The Young Turk Revolution of 1908, for example, seems to correspond to the bloodless variety known in Peru as a *telegráfico*. Its only two

12

victims were a young officer whom the conspirators suspected of being a stool pigeon (he was kidnapped and murdered with the active participation of his brother-in-law Enver) and one of Abdülhamid's generals shot in broad daylight in the market square of Monastir. The constitutional revolution itself was accomplished by a flood of telegrams that rained upon the Sultan's palace from army commanders, political committees, and provincial governors throughout Macedonia. Only a year later did the Macedonian army march upon the capital to quell a counterrevolutionary mutiny among the Istanbul garrison. A uniquely painless way of accomplishing a military coup was devised in Iraq in 1938: a discreet ultimatum whispered into the premier's ear at a social gathering resulted in the cabinet's resignation only hours later.[5] This last incident, however, reflected a situation where the army for some time had called the tune for the habitual musical-chair game of cabinet formation within the Iraqi oligarchy.

At other times, a determined show of force by the army is required to overthrow a government. Bakr Sidqi's coup in 1936 involved five airplanes dropping quantities of leaflets over Baghdad—as well as four bombs that took a total of seven casualties. More commonly, army units occupy key communications points around the capital—road junctions, the radio station, the royal or presidential palace, and the government offices. This, with some variation, was the story of the revolutions in Cairo in 1952, in Bagdad in 1958, and in Turkey in 1960. The decisive military phases of the coup are likely to involve little cost of lives: only fools will barehandedly oppose machine guns, tanks, or bombers. The bloodier phases of a military revolution are likely to be the result of deliberate subsequent action, as Bakr Sidqi's murder of the previous war minister and the death sentences imposed on Menderes and a few associates after a year-long trial, or else of an enraged civilian mob tolerated by the army, as in the ferocious massacre in Baghdad in 1958.

The military leaders of most coups solemnly announce that they will not take power for themselves or will return it to civilian hands quickly; yet few live up to that initial promise. Here again the record shows a variety of patterns. A refusal by the military conspirators to take office creates an unstable situation where power is divorced from responsibility, and further coups are the logical sequel. The seven Iraqi coups of the 1936-41 period consisted in as many changes in civilian cabinets enforced by military threats. The very fact that the first such army coup had succeeded in bringing one faction to power created a temptation, or even compulsion, for its opponents to use the same tactics. A chain reaction of coups was the result; and, while it lasted, cabinets were in effect responsible neither to the monarch nor the parliament, let alone the electorate, but rather to informal combinations of key generals and colonels. (In February, 1940, one cabinet was ousted as a result of a vote of five to three at one such gathering.) In Syria in 1949, and again from 1954 to 1957, one might be tempted to speak of a Gresham's law of military intervention. Any army coup, unless carried out by the chief of staff himself, will disrupt the discipline and cohesiveness of the officer corps. Once a few generals and colonels have succeeded in seizing power, any aspiring major or captain will soon nurse similar ambitions.

In the recent Egyptian and Turkish revolutions, the military rulers proclaimed their hopes of quickly remedying the evils of the previous regime and of re-establishing an era of civilian normalcy. In each case the sequel exposed the fallacy of this one-shot intervention theory, whether or not sincerely espoused. Nagib and Nasir replaced Faruq with a regency council for his infant son and invited the Egyptian parties to purge themselves of corrupt elements. After some months, they concluded that corruption had been more than skin-deep and that no trained, clean cadres stood ready to take over. With Nasir's victory over Nagib, the initial promise of early elections was dropped altogether.[6] In Turkey, General Gürsel at first thought his task accomplished upon the arrest of the president, premier, and cabinet of the *ancien régime* and the appointment of a commission of law professors to draft a new constitution. The professors pointed out to him that Menderes' dictatorial regime had had the solid support of parliament and the Democratic party, and insisted that the parliamentarians be arrested and the party suppressed. And the learned jurists proved utterly unable to deliver on their over-confident promise of a new constitution within a month. In the end, it took well over a year to get a new constitution adopted, a new parliament elected, and a civilian cabinet formed. The more ambitious tasks envisaged by the National Unity Committee—such as the restoration of the economy, the currency, and public morality—still remain on the agenda of their suc-

14

cessors. There were indications, moreover, that continued army pressure was required to bring about the incongruous coalition of pro- and anti-Menderes forces that took office in November, 1961; and the abortive coup of March, 1962, again revealed that the political involvement of the military was not yet at an end. The future alone can tell whether the army can henceforth safely withdraw from the political arena.

Finally, *there are often widening rifts within the military junta installed by a coup.* The Egyptian, Iraqi, and Turkish juntas all consisted of officers with the rank of colonel or below, who planned the actual conspiracy, and were supplemented by older generals who were co-opted as respected figureheads or leader figures. The general in each case turned out to be more conservative than his juniors—Nagib insisted on early party elections while Nasir wished to perpetuate the Revolutionary Command Council; Qasim resisted Arif's plans for union with the U.A.R.; Gürsel opposed Türkeş's vague ideas of radical social reform under authoritarian military aegis. These three examples also show that the dispute may be resolved either way: in Egypt, the younger radicals won out; in Iraq and Turkey, they lost, at least in the initial round.

THE EFFECTS OF MILITARY INTERVENTION

Having surveyed the cultural and natural history of Middle Eastern military coups, it remains to survey briefly their effects. The authors of a study of Latin American politics hold that "the armed forces are probably the single most serious impediment to the development of democracy."[7] Another political scientist has argued with equal confidence that, in the Southeast Asia of the 1960's, military dictatorships represent the best hope for the survival and development of free representative institutions.[8] There may be special conditions that make these sweeping judgments more nearly applicable to the regions for which they first were formulated. For the Middle East, at least, any such monistic interpretations should be firmly rejected. There are armies and armies, and there are military coups and military coups. The one thing all military regimes have in common is that, by their very definition, they have a certain amount of coercive power at their disposal—and even in this respect there are important differences in degree. How they will apply that power and what fruits they will reap depend on their own character and the setting in which they operate.

One obvious and fundamental distinction is that betwen armies based on universal military training—as in Israel, Turkey, Egypt, Syria, and more recently Iraq—and those based on volunteers—as in Iran, Jordan, Saudi Arabia, and Yemen. The conscript armies can serve as an important factor in economic and social development—through training in literacy as in Turkey, or in the national language as in Israel, or through the communication of mechanical, industrial, or even agricultural skills. In these same countries, the officer corps generally is selected upon an egalitarian basis, given professionalized training, and promoted by merit. Where an army with such an officer corps takes power, it is likely to pursue goals of political reform, social modernization, and economic development. How well it will succeed is quite a different matter. Colonel Nasir, for example, must try to reverse a steady decline in Egyptian living standards due to limited resources and a heavy rate of population increase—a problem that would tax the ingenuity of any government, military or civil. General Gürsel's Committee of National Unity was handicapped by the astounding political naïveté of an officer corps long insulated from participation in the civilian political process. On the other hand, the armies of the surviving monarchies of the Middle East clearly serve as props to traditional autocratic or oligarchic regimes. The Iranian army, in particular, which boasts the highest ratio of officers to enlisted men of any Middle Eastern country,[9] has long been known for endemic corruption and favoritism. Unless such an army is itself drastically reformed, it would be idle to expect it to serve as the spearhead of social progress.

It should be noted at this point that the distinction between military coups and military revolutions must properly rest not upon any difference in the technique by which power is seized but rather upon the scope and success of the reform program which is subsequently enacted. All military revolutions begin as coups: the seizure of power out of civilian hands must follow certain rules determined by the prevailing technology of the political and military organizations. In turn, the proclamations that accompany the coup tend to reflect the political philosophy popular at the time and place. In the mid–twentieth century, any serious claimant to power, regardless of his antecedents, associations, or intentions, will justify his claim by professing profound concern for national independence, for popular aspirations, for social justice, and for economic development. Once power is attained, some coups evolve into revolutions. The difference is not in the promise but in the performance.

The most decisive factor is the relationship of the military to the civilian segment of the political process. That a great variety of configurations here is possible within the same over-all setting and period is illustrated by the final years of the Ottoman Empire. The revolutionaries of 1908 were content to see Abdülhamid reproclaim the constitution he had blithely disregarded in three decades of despotic rule and replace the most obnoxious of his ministers with bureaucrats of a more liberal tinge. In 1909, the same revolutionary group insisted on Abdülhamid's deposition, a revision of the monarchic constitution along parliamentary lines, and the appointment of cabinets subservient to the Union and Progress party. Enver's raid on the Sublime Porte in 1913 brought to power the youthful Unionist hotheads who made a mockery of the electoral process and plunged the country into disastrous defeat in World War I, but who at the same time undertook a series of courageous administrative, legal, fiscal, and educational changes that laid the groundwork for the reform program of the following decades. Finally, Mustafa Kemal's Defense of Rights movement combined the local civilian organizations left behind by the Unionists with a military apex, won an impressive military and diplomatic victory, created a party and a state in which the military could once again withdraw from politics, and undertook his sweeping legal, social, and cultural transformation.

The Turkish experience under Kemal suggests specifically that after a period of profound military involvement in politics, a conscious decision by the leading general-turned-politician may be the most effective way of re-establishing the separation of civilian and military affairs. Any soldiers who are disinclined to return to their barracks from conviction are more likely to do so from habitual obedience to a prestigious commander.[10]

In conclusion it may be well to point out that the neat distinction drawn throughout this essay between civilian and military politics is somewhat artificial. Until the eighteenth century, there had been no such systematic differentiation in the Middle East or, for that matter, in continental Europe. The sultans of the classical period led their armies into the field in person. The *ulama* (or learned men in Islamic law and theology) had always formed a clearly distinct class; but the empire's civil and military servants—governors, army commanders, judges, ministers—had received the same initial training in the sultan's palace school, and shifts among these careers were common. In most periods of recorded history, the maintenance of armed forces has constituted the irreducible minimum of government. Other public functions such as taxation, education, public works, and social services began either as subsidiary activities or were added as subsequent luxuries. In new countries or at times of internal and external crisis, the lines again become blurred in various ways. In Kemalist Turkey, army officers were barred from sitting in—and even voting for—parliament. Yet former officers filled many of the key positions in the government and in the Republican People's party; the chief of staff held a position independent of ministerial control; generals on active duty continued to double up as provincial governors; and during prolonged periods of siege (in the Kurdish provinces in the 1920's and in Istanbul throughout World War II), civil authority was subordinated to military command. In the early mandate days of Iraq and Syria, centralized administration had to be established by military force. In Israel, defense considerations tend to dominate economic and social planning, and there have been complaints that Prime Minister Ben-Gurion's long tenure as minister of defense has shielded the armed forces from effective civilian control.

Nevertheless, the very complexity of modern government tends toward a reassertion of the distinction between military and civilian affairs. This is seen both in coups, which consist in a mere change of top political leadership, and in military revolutions, which result in more profound political and social transformations. One of the greatest assets of the military in a coup is their reputation for honesty, decisiveness, and efficiency, which, in the eyes of a discontented populace, contrasts favorably with the corruption and inefficiency of the ousted civilian government. But, the officers were efficient while serving the single, simple purpose of national defense. Moving into the unfamiliar political scene, which is by definition an arena of conflicting purposes, and dealing with complex subjects of financial, industrial, or agricultural

18

planning for which they are entirely untrained, the officers may quickly lose their good reputation. In fact, the more extravagant the initial popular enthusiasm, the keener and quicker the disappointment. At this point the stage is set for another military coup (on the facile assumption that the military are indeed uncorrupt and efficient, but the leaders of the first coup happened to be the exception that proves the rule) or, at length, for a return to civilian government (once the military reputation is thoroughly tarnished).

In a military revolution, the officers stay in power longer but the very magnitude of a reform program forces them to sever their active connection with the army. Mustafa Kemal, throughout most of the Turkish War of Independence, relinquished active command at the front in order to preside over the deliberations of the truculent and fractious National Assembly at Ankara. Similarly the colonels and majors in Nasir's Revolutionary Command Council and Gürsel's Committee of National Unity could not continue in command of their regiments or battalions while taking charge of ministries, directorates-general, and provincial governorships. It therefore becomes largely a matter of conceptual definition whether Egypt, a decade after the 1952 revolution, is said to be governed by the military or by a group of civilian ex-officers initially propelled into power by armed force. The shift from military to civilian control is apparent in the fact that Kemal, after the formation of the First Republic, based his support on the Republican People's party—the first Middle Eastern political movement with a farflung constituency organization. Nasir's National Union is an attempt in the same direction.

Only the future can tell whether Nasir in Egypt or Qasim in Iraq will be able to match Kemal's achievement of re-establishing civilian supremacy. In any case, the ultimate success of a military regime depends on its skill in allowing or promoting the rise of effective civilian institutions that will render future military intervention superfluous—in short, in fostering a set of political rules whereby clubs no longer will be trumps.

1. Samuel P. Huntington, surveying the military scene since 1945, observes aptly, "The inhibition of direct intergovernmental violence contrasted with the frequency and variety of violence in the domestic politics of colonial territories and independent states of Latin America, Africa, the Middle East, and southern

Asia. These were the principal military arenas in world politics." *Changing Patterns of Military Politics* ("International Yearbook of Political Behavior Research," No. 3 [Glencoe, Ill., 1962]), p. 18.

2. Thomas Hobbes, *English Works*, ed. Molesworth, VI, 122. The above was written before the September, 1962, military coup in Yemen.

3. Gamal Abdul Nasser, *Egypt's Liberation: Philosophy of the Revolution* (Washington D. C., 1955), p. 81.

4. The above two paragraphs are taken from my article, "The Army and the Founding of the Turkish Republic," *World Politics*, XI, No. 4 (July, 1959), 514 f. The phrase "ruling institution" is that of Albert Lybyer, *The Government of the Ottoman Empire* (Cambridge, Mass., 1913); the metaphor of the "cutting edge" that of Lewis V. Thomas, in L. V. Thomas and R. N. Frye, *The United States and Turkey and Iran* (Cambridge, Mass., 1951), p. 51.

5. See Majid Khadduri, *Independent Iraq 1932-1958* (2nd ed.; London, 1960), p. 133.

6. On the gradual transformation of the Egyptian regime, see the informative study by P. J. Vatikiotis, *The Egyptian Army in Politics* (Bloomington, Ind., 1961), especially pp. 71-96.

7. Charles O. Porter and Robert J. Alexander, *The Struggle for Democracy in Latin America* (New York, 1961), p. 46.

8. Guy J. Pauker, "Southeast Asia as a Problem Area in the Next Decade," *World Politics*, XI, No. 3 (July, 1959), 325-45.

9. One to fourteen against one to twenty in Pakistan and Jordan and one to forty-eight in Tunisia. See Manfred Halpern's chapter in John J. Johnson (ed.), *The Political Role of the Army in Underdeveloped Areas* (Princeton, N. J., 1962), p. 292-95, which contains a convenient table giving details of size, recruitment, and training of Middle Eastern armies and their officers.

10. For details of the relative disengagement of the army from the politics of the First Turkish Republic, see my article cited *supra, note* 4, especially pp. 543-51.

The Role of the Military in Society and Government in Turkey*

SYDNEY NETTLETON FISHER

GHAZI MUSTAFA KEMAL PASHA, victorious general over Greeks and the Allies after World War I, and later known as Atatürk, became the first president of the Turkish Republic and was re-elected three times. Ismet Pasha, victorious general at two decisive battles in the War of Independence, and later known as Inönü, succeeded to the presidency upon Atatürk's death and was twice re-elected. In 1961, General Cemal Gürsel was elected as the fourth president, after having served for nearly seventeen months as Head of State of the Interim Government.

Under Atatürk, Inönü served as Prime Minister for thirteen years; and under President Gürsel, he is Prime Minister again. In addition, Atatürk and Inönü have been the heads of the Republican People's party. The leader of the National party in the late 1940's was Marshal Fevzi Çakmak, for years the army chief of staff; and General Ragip Gümüşpala was head of the Justice party, which recently captured

*The author is greatly indebted to the Social Science Research Council for a grant that permitted him to reside and travel in Turkey in 1958-59 and renew his older contacts and thus obtain fresh viewpoints on the development of society and government, many of which are expressed in this paper. The Council is in no way responsible for any opinions presented here.

21

more seats in the newly elected Senate than did General Inönü's Republican People's party and stood second to that party in the new National Assembly. Only in the decade of the 1950's was there a government without a general as president or prime minister; and that regime of the Democrat party succumbed to a military coup d'état, with Prime Minister Adnan Menderes eventually being hanged, and President Celal Bayar having his death sentence commuted to life imprisonment because of his advanced years. Considering the history of the Turkish Republic over the last forty years, one could well assume that leadership in politics and participation and/or interference in government are significant and successful extra-curricular activities of the Turkish military.

If Professor Speiser's theory [1] of the *ethneme* in historical development of society is correct, then the more recent role of the military in society and government in Turkey should have been readily expected. Almost as far back in Turkish history as one may wish to delve, the well-known leaders of society have been military men. With respect to the development of the Turks of Asia Minor, the occupation resulted from military action; and subsequent tribal, family, and dynastic rivalries were maintained or resolved by military action, a significant role for the military in government. Professor Wittek greatly enlightens the subject and importance of ghazi participation in advances of the Seljuk and Ottoman Turks.[2] These paramilitary fraternal orders guaranteed that the military exercised a dominant voice in society. Certainly, the depth and persistence of ghazi influence were attested by the title "Ghazi" that devolved upon Kemal by popular acclaim in the 1920's.

Even before the conquest of Constantinople, the government had been beset by military figures intriguing to influence affairs, as is revealed by the difficulties the young Mehmed II witnessed. Later, these pressures and roles were magnified: Bayezid II had to declare a favored position for the military; Selim I was placed in power by their support; and Suleiman executed two of his sons because of military intrigues. European envoys in their reports from the Sublime Porte were unanimous in regard to military influence upon governmental policies. In time its only rivalry came from the women of the palace. Accordingly, the military became unduly conservative, verging upon a reactionary course.

22

Civilians, both in and out of government, were, nevertheless, not entirely ignored in early Ottoman society since the foundations of law and society were rooted in Islamic theology. The word "mufti" portrays the significance of the civilian in Islamic society and, to a certain degree, this division of the military and civilian in Ottoman affairs was defined in Professor Lybyer's description of the Ruling and Muslim Institutions.[3] As extensions of the frontiers became more difficult and less profitable, the prestige of the civilian advanced and many of the military turned to other pursuits. Ghazis hid on their estates when campaign drums were beaten, and janissaries became candymakers and pastry cooks, being soldiers only on payday.

Caught in this slough of low esteem, the military took refuge behind wholly reactionary and bigoted positions, whereas a number of leading civilians, exposed to aspects of eighteenth century French Enlighten-ment, deplored the stagnation about them and advocated a regeneration of Turkish society. Taking cues from Russian and Austrian armies, and especially from military agents of French Revolutionary governments and Napoleon, a few of the Turkish military were disposed to become modernized. But it took the Greek Revolt and Mahmud II's destruction of the janissaries in 1826 to open the way for a more thorough revitalization of the Turkish military. Nevertheless, military evolution proceeded slowly in the nineteenth century, and civilian aspects of societal development more than kept pace.

In a very real sense, the story of the current entanglement of the Turkish military in society and government follows the humiliation of the Congress of Berlin and the loss of so much Balkan territory, and begins with the tyranny of Abdul Hamid II. All that went before only conditioned the Turkish people for the episodes of the last eighty years. The sultan was not anxious to educate a populace to rebel but he had to have an army. Military academies were subsidized and staffed by competent European instructors, many from the new German Empire. Here the young cadets learned German and/or French, a media that came equipped with an open window to a rapidly moving, industrious, prosperous, stimulating, free society.

Resentful of the inferior position of Turkey, of Turks, and of the Turkish military, particularly after the Mürzsteg Program brought wider contacts and obviously unfavorable visual comparisons with

European officers, young Turkish officers conspired with dissident intellectuals to bring on the Young Turk Revolution of 1908. As Dr. Ramsaur has shown, in his work on the Young Turks,[4] class after class at Harbiye, the Military Academy, was permeated by the revolutionary spirit, a feeling also widespread at the Naval Academy, the Artillery and Engineering School, the Military Medical School, the Veterinary School, and the Civil College where government officials were trained. At the Army Staff College, Von der Goltz Pasha instilled in the young officers German ideas of responsibility and national leadership, whereas the spirit hardly passed through the gates of the University of Istanbul, long a citadel of the old order. Enver, Kemal, and Ismet were Harbiye cadets and graduates of the Army Staff College in 1903, 1904, and 1906, respectively; they became convinced that the old order had to go if Turkey was to survive in the modern world. All were patriots, angry at corruption, ignorance, poverty, the sultan's spies, the material want of the army and navy, the frozen mentality of religious leaders, and the special privileges of foreigners in Turkey. Somewhat naïvely, they believed the ousting of Abdul Hamid II would introduce the millenium. Thus, the Turkish military pulled off its first coup d'état of this century. When Abdul Hamid II's reactionary counterrevolution, the following spring, toppled the Young Turks, the military rescued them with a second coup d'état.

How successful this new regime might have been is debatable, for world events embroiled them with actions that precluded freedom for maneuver. The Italian War, the Balkan Wars, and World War I filled seven of the ten years of the Young Turks, and Enver made a wrong guess when he allied with Germany in 1914. The Armistice of 1918 was followed by such frightful ineptitudes and stupidities on the part of the Western Powers that most Turks chose to follow the course charted by those military leaders the Allies did not suppress.

Out of this came the disestablishment of the Ottoman sultan in 1922, a miraculous feat performed by Kemal and his military friends. Although not exactly a coup d'état, the sultan fled on a British man-of-war after the Kemalists had won effective control of the land as well as the hearts of the people.

From this military seizure of power, the third of the twentieth century, the First Republic was born.[5] Of the thirteen leaders in this move-

24

ment cited by an outstanding scholar of the period,[6] seven were graduates of the Army Staff College, one of the Naval Academy, and one of the Medical College. Of the remaining four, one attended the Veterinary School until imprisoned by the sultan for subversive activities, two studied in French schools, and one was graduated from an American college. Behind these leaders were other military men occupying positions in cabinets, ministries, parliament, and key offices of the government. The Republic was controlled by army officers in civilian garb. They continued to think as military men, but more importantly they maintained close liaison with their fellow officers remaining in the army and with whom a firm two-way confidence was retained and strengthened.

These officials and officers were steeped in a new Turkish basic nationalist ideal, conceived from the French Revolution, sifted and tested by the Young Turks, and defined and organized by the great Turkish sociologist Ziya Gökalp who preached, "We belong to the Turkish nation, the Muslim religious community and the European civilization."[7] He popularized the slogan "Turkification, Islamization, Modernization." Kemal and his cohorts subscribed to these ideals which, after some modification, were molded and condensed into Kemal's six points: republicanism, nationalism, populism, secularism, statism, and reformism. Using these six arrows in his quiver, Kemal attacked the problem of creating a new state.

A great majority of active adult persons today in Turkey received their education and passed through their formative years in those two decades under Atatürk. Of the thirty-eight junta members [8] who were chosen by their fellow officers to lead the recent coup, only one, General Cemal Gürsel, belonged to the older group, he having been born in 1895. It should be remembered, moreover, that he was not one of the instigators of the conspiracy but joined shortly before the day of the coup. A few of the others, in their early fifties, had passed through military schools in the late 1920's; the great bulk of the group that came to be called the National Unity Committee was born in the years between 1915 and 1925; one as late as 1933. To many, many students in that era of Atatürk, his six points were as important as the Ten Commandments, and it was a common sight to see on coat lapels a small button shield on which the six arrows were emblazoned.

Very likely, most of these military leaders as youths were wearing such insignia twenty-five years ago. What did Atatürk and Inönü tell them these arrows meant? Books have been, and are being, written on each of these points so there is no need to elaborate.[9] It was axiomatic that Turkey was a republic, and leaders of that day were most familiar with the Third French Republic; the lessons of Boulanger and the military role in the Dreyfuss Affair had not been lost on them. To Atatürk, a republic meant a government controlled by civilians; only on rare occasions was he pictured in military dress; usually he wore an ordinary business suit or white tie and tails. Officers serving in civilian posts had to resign irrevocably from the military services, a move which many came to regret when the vagaries of political maneuvering dealt them out. In a republic the army was supposed to stay out of politics. In Turkey, officers did not have the vote. This concept became so well instilled into the political ideology of the educated elite that, as the days of the National Unity Committee's rule lengthened into weeks, months, and more than a year, civilian groups in Ankara, Istanbul, and other cities turned their backs as the military passed by.

Atatürk's second arrow, nationalism, at first view appeared straight and simple enough. "Turkey for the Turks, and the Turks for Turkey" was on everyone's tongue and easy to understand. The Young Turks, before and after 1908, debated nationalism in terms of Pan-Islamism and Ottomanism. Intellectuals such as Ziya Gökalp, Abdullah Cevdet, Hüseyn Cahid, Halide Edib, Yusuf Akçura, and Ahmet Ağaoğlu eventually rejected both of these and accepted Pan-Turkism as the only feasible nationalism for modern Turkey. Akçura,[10] a Tatar from Russia, studied in Paris where he became imbued with German racial theories and French national ideologies, especially those of Ernest Renan and Maurice Barrès. In a most significant article in a Turkish newspaper published in Cairo in 1904, Akçura declared that Pan-Turkism was the only way. These new Pan-Turkish nationalists advocated purging from Turkish life all foreign and pernicious influences, reviving the old Turkish culture of Asia, and purifying the Turkish language by casting out Arabic and Persian loan words.

On the other hand, Ziya Gökalp,[11] a devotee of Emile Durkheim, felt the impact of the defeats in Libya and in the Balkan Wars and thus, almost suddenly, became painfully aware of western Europe progress

26

and advance. He solved the dilemma by drawing a distinction between culture and civilization and proposing the adoption of Western civilization while preserving and refining purely Turkish culture. Atatürk, the pragmatist, ignored the parodox and preserved, even intensified, the dichotomy. Without question, Turkey moved Westward in most aspects of national life and, as one contributor to this volume has observed, the Swiss Civil and Italian Criminal Codes were referred to as the Turkish Civil and Turkish Criminal Codes; the hat, white tie, and tails were not Western in mode but the dress of civilized nations, and the Western calendar was an international one.[12] Westernization was hard on the morale, and school boys were sensitive to the question of imitation of the West. It should not be forgotten that the officers leading the coup d'état of 1960 were school boys then.

To maintain Turkish pride and to make these Western innovations somewhat more palatable, Atatürk turned to Akçura's Turkism and concocted the National History and Sun-Language theories. The former proposed that civilized man had originated in Central Asia, and, since the Turkish homeland was Central Asia, it seemed valid to state that the Turks had been the first civilized men. Adam was the first man; the Turkish word *"adam"* means "man"; therefore, Adam was a Turk. In any case, the theory ran that Sumerians, Hittites, Greeks, Latins, Germans, English, Chinese, and all other peoples were from the same Turkish stock, were ancestors and/or cousins of the Turks, and had forgotten their origins. Only Turks had remained true Turks. The Sun-Language theory asserted that Turks had invented the spoken word and all other languages were Turkish derivatives. Turkish historians found acceptance rather difficult but with Atatürk himself addressing international Sun-Language congresses in Istanbul, quiet approval was the better part of wisdom. As one wise Middle Eastern historian[13] remarked, "It may not be true, but it is hard to disprove."

Populism meant the wiping out of all class privileges and distinctions —a kind of egalitarianism. In essence and in its finality, it meant Western democracy. In the 1930's, a leading Turkish sociologist wrote of populism, "In the most crucial and agitated hour of its existence a society's strongest social foundation is its sturdy selfconsciousness."[14] Populism belonged to the future, for Atatürk's revolution, although dramatically attacking social custom, hardly altered the social structure

27

of Turkey. Universal education, as one aspect of populism, was ardently preached; new schools were built by the thousands but never enough so that each village could boast of one; and normal schools were not able to train enough teachers to fill those that did exist.

Kemal usually was regarded as an atheist; he may have been one privately, but in his public policy he could better be labeled anti-clerical in the manner of French, Germans, and Italians at the turn of the century. Religious aspects were removed from schools and dress; beards were cut; tekkes and turbes closed; and fasting during Ramazan was out-of-fashion. Atatürk fervently believed that Islam, as a popular religion, had frozen many centuries earlier and had prevented the populace of Turkey from entering the twentieth century. Not only was the state to be freed from the shackles of religion, but religious superstition had to be erased from the hearts and minds of all Turks.

With the worldwide depression of the 1930's the government assumed an active role in industrialization, in exploitation of national resources, and in stimulation of the growth of the national economy. For political reasons, statism was said to bolster private enterprise but more truly it advanced state capitalism. Whatever it was, statism led the way for a perceptible rise in the standard of living in Turkey, especially in the cities.

Lastly, Atatürk swore that his revolution was a continuous and evolutionary process. Reform became the watchword and there was to be no resting on the oars, even after he was dead.

But the effects of these six campaigns on the Turks were not spread evenly. In Ankara, Istanbul, Izmir, and a few other larger cities, innovations were noticeable to the most casual tourist. More importantly, the spirit, if not the fact, infected a majority of provincial towns, especially among people who were maturing in the 1930's. After the adoption of the new alphabet in 1928, school books were all rewritten and filled with Kemalism. The youth of the small towns idealized Atatürk and his reforms. The villages, however, were barely touched; religion, illiteracy, standards of living, and society remained static.

In addition to the quandry over Westernization and the orientation of Turkish civilization and culture, there arose under Atatürk a dilemma with respect to the status of the military man and the place of the army in society. Gökalp had praised the virtues of the soldier and

28

had adhered to the philosophy that the Turkish soldier and the Turkish armed forces through the centuries were important and glorious components in fashioning the resolute character of Turkism. Turks, especially in the provinces, subscribed heartily to this idea and were ever proud of the army's exploits and exceedingly deferential to men in uniform. The respect generated by the appearance of a general or any officer at a gathering or anywhere in public was genuine and was a sign of the peculiar nationalism of the Kemalist era.

On the other hand, few, if any, sons from families of even moderate means ever thought of the military as a career. Atatürk was playing down militarism and boys sought an education for business, engineering, law, medicine, dentistry, government service, the foreign service, anything but the army or navy. Still, there were not enough schools and only the fortunate could choose. Hence, a poor boy or a middle-class son from a more remote part of Anatolia might be able to obtain an education only in a professional military school.

Considerations such as this brief digression regarding the place of the military in contemporary Turkish society are not without point, for early on the morning of May 27, 1960, the National Unity Committee, a small group of officers bound together in a conspiracy, took over the government, both in Ankara and Istanbul, and locked up the leaders of the Democrat party. Referring to Bayar, Menderes, and others, one Committee member [15] said, "In 1950 I viewed and knew them as patriotic and good men, after 1954 as persons who acted according to their own understandings, but after 1957 as persons who trampled on the laws and worked only for the realization of their own wishes and interests." Some of the officers had begun the plot several years before the coup, and an official of a friendly foreign government attended, as an observer, a secret meeting in a Western capital. General Cemal Gürsel, who joined the group in its later days, was recognized as the new Head of State but by no means the absolute master of the Committee, since on a number of occasions shortly after May 27, the Committee required his public retraction of independent statements. On June 12, the identity of the thirty-eight members of the National Unity Committee was revealed along with a new Provisional Constitution which the NUC had drafted with the assistance of three university law professors. The Constitution provided that the NUC would lose

29

its legal existence and dissolve automatically on the day a new Grand National Assembly should be elected.

When asked if the officers were not fearful of the plot's failure, one remarked,[16] "We knew the nation was thirsty for freedom," and another [17] quoted Tevfik Fikret, "Free thought, free conscience, free culture." University students and military cadets had been demonstrating against the old regime; newspaper editors were in jail; and opposition political leaders, their movements restricted, were under house surveillance or arrest. The enthusiasm for the revolt among the educated elite of Turkey spread rapidly, and one youth wrote to American friends on June 11, "There had not been such a time in my life when I felt so wonderfully happy and proud. . . . do you realize how great it is for my country . . . Cemal Gursel will [not] become a Fidel Castro. . . . it is not done by [the] Army alone. The University has 11 [sic] Martyrs. I could have been one for I was together with them and two got shot right in front of me. We earned what we have now. And no other man can try to do the things Democrats and Menderes's government had done to us. We are hopefully and happily looking ahead to our future. God be with us. Freedom and peace we want and we deserve it."[18]

Who were these thirty-eight? Five were generals, and among the twenty-six staff officers there were eight colonels between thirty-nine and forty-five years of age, five lieutenant colonels between thirty-seven and forty-three, nine majors between thirty-five and forty-five, three navy captains and one lieutenant commander between thirty-one and thirty-seven. The non-staff officers included three majors, two captains, one naval lieutenant, and one gendarmery captain.[19] Many of these occupied key posts in the military establishment. General Gürsel had been commander of land forces; General Özdilek was commander of the First Army and martial law commander in Istanbul; Lieutenant Colonel Karaman was chief of the staff branch of the General Staff with the responsibility of assigning generals and staff officers to their posts; Colonel Köksal was commander of the guard regiment that protected Bayar, Menderes, and other high governmental officials; General Madanoğlu was commander of the Twenty-eighth Division, which controlled Ankara; Colonel Türkeş was commander of the Co-ordination Section of the NATO armed forces; and General Ulay was commandant

30

of the Military Academy in Ankara and had been Turkish military attaché in Cairo at the time of the overthrow of King Faruq by the RCC. Since Turkish soldiers obey their officers, NUC was in a position of strength. Still, who were they? A very few were born and grew up in Istanbul and Izmir; the vast majority were from provincial towns or villages. Several were sons of military men, most were from artisan or lower-middle-class families. All were poor: one, at the age of thirteen, ran away from a poverty-stricken home in the mountains of eastern Anatolia, made his way in near rags in freezing temperatures across country to Erzincan where he was one of eight to pass entrance examinations to the military school. One was born in Cyprus, and another came from the village of Akseki in the Taurus Mountains, a spot so barren and stony that one has to see it to believe it could exist. Another's family fell on hard times during World War II, forcing the lad to be a shepherd for more than a year. Three were born in what is now Greece and were transferred, as small children, in the population exchanges after the War of Independence. Several, of course, were fatherless at an early age and had to make their own way entirely.

There are a number of military lycées in Turkey but over half of the thirty-eight studied at Kuleli Military Lycée. It would be interesting to know what the teachers at Kuleli taught the boys. It reminds one of the old school tie. Most of them stood at the top of their classes and all were thoroughly imbued with Atatürk's program. From military lycées they went on to military academies, the War College, and staff schools. They became well educated men and as such, along with a great many other educated Turks, rapidly became disabused with the political and national programs of the Democrat regime.

Perhaps because of their origins, but more likely because of their frequent and close contacts with villages and villagers, military officers experienced first hand the wide chasm that existed and widened between the village peasant and the educated, urbane, and sophisticated modern Turk of Ankara and Istanbul. Their respective societies were centuries apart. Turkish officers in reading of foreign cultures and the modern world and in seeing these for themselves in their foreign assignments were shocked and impatient when they contemplated conditions at home. Most humiliating of all were their comparisons of Turkish and Balkan villages. Believing that one hundred years ago the two

31

had been comparable, officers found it galling to note that the Balkans had literacy rates as high as 75 per cent while Turkish rates seemed stationary.

Everything seemed out-of-joint. Menderes and his party were busy and talked about attacking every problem. Yet, the economy was strained; common articles were either rationed or unobtainable, except on the black market; the press was muzzled; religious obscurantism was encouraged and subsidized; and corruption was rife. It appeared that progress and Atatürk's reforms were forgotten, and the opinion developed that "those seeking votes cannot undertake reforms and cannot even keep their promises." [20] That old cliché "familiarity breeds contempt" worked well in the case of those highly placed officers who came into daily touch with the politicians. After the coup, one officer [21] observed how pitiful politicians were: Bayar inquired about his salary; Koraltan kept asking every few minutes if he was to be killed; and poor Menderes stood up every time his jailor or a guard entered his cell. How petty and unsoldierlike in the face of adversity!

"Where do we go from here?" might well have been the question on the lips of the 38 within a day or two after the coup, and it certainly was a major topic in their discussions five or six months later. They had no thought of establishing a long-term military rule nor any intention of permitting a dictator to arise. They were even wary of the idea of one man becoming too prominent, reminiscent of the experience of the Egyptian RCC and Nagib and Nasir. The idea was to rid Turkey of the rascals and to get the reforms of Atatürk back again on the tracks. Since the old constitution had not prevented Democrat abuses, it was to be replaced by a new one that would usher in the Second Turkish Republic.

Sixteen days after the successful coup, the Provisional Constitution was promulgated by NUC. It provided that the president of the NUC be Head of State, Head of the Government, and commander in chief. Ministers of the Interim Government to be appointed by the President of the NUC might be members of the NUC or impartial citizens who had no political party affiliations as of May 27. The NUC was empowered to supervise cabinet ministers at all times or to relieve them of their functions. Laws were proposed by the cabinet or by members of the NUC and approved by the NUC, following which the Head of

State was required to promulgate or veto them within ten days; a four-fifths majority of the NUC could override a veto. Words did not mince the question of authority.

Members of the NUC had very positive views with respect to how the state should progress and the role of the government in furthering and channeling this advance. A novel, *Ince Memed,* by Yaşar Kemal, now available in English under the title, *Memed, My Hawk,*[22] appeared in 1956 and had a marked influence upon members of the Committee. This is the story of a village boy in the southern mountain area of Anatolia and his struggle against the hardships of life and the conservative land-owning class. Penned in most vivid language and vigorous style, the life of Memed brought home the reality and sincerity of village poverty and primitive conditions with such force that almost every committeeman has admitted in public and private conversations the impact of *Ince Memed* upon his thinking.

Other books that have had wide influence on the junta include *Çalikuşu (The Autobiography of a Turkish Girl)* and *Beyaz Zambaklar Memleketinde (In the Country of the White Lilies),* the latter being a fanciful portrayal of life in a society more perfect than found in present-day Turkey. All of the thirty-eight, as educated Turks, are familiar with one or more foreign languages and are acquainted with a wide range of European and American writers and publications, including Nietzsche, Abraham Lincoln, *Les Misérables,* Pearl Buck, the *New York Times,* Jaurès, Pushkin, Tolstoy, and, interestingly, the most socially minded indicated in various statements considerable familiarity with *Time* magazine.

What did they preach? Educational mobilization by sending all officer candidates to the villages to teach for eighteen months; religious and moral training for the entire nation; cultural development and the re-establishment of the Village Institutes for total welfare of the nation; modern dress for women; elimination of poverty and the wiping out of the shacks, slums, and tin-can villages around Istanbul and other cities; land reform, on the one hand, to prevent fragmentization of land holdings among a peasant's numerous heirs and, on the other, to break up the extensive holdings of *derebeys* and *ağas* in the east such as depicted in *Ince Memed;* industrialization of the country to raise living standards; continuation of the linguistic reforms aban-

33

THE MILITARY IN THE MIDDLE EAST

doned on Atatürk's death; control of investment to combat waste of resources; prevention and treatment of disease and the inauguration of a program of health insurance similar to that of the British; provision of job opportunities for all; reforestation of Turkey; and the introduction of new measures to insure tax justice for every profession and class.[23] Anyone familiar with modern Turkish problems will understand from the scope of these programs that the Turkish military were cognizant of the society in which they lived. The fundamental cause of the May 27 action was the military's concern with the ills of the society and the belief that the officials of the government were irresponsible, negligent, venal, and perfidious. Now the job was up to the thirty-eight and the new government they created.

Running a government is quite a different matter from criticizing or overthrowing it. The cabinet, instituted the day following the coup, was legalized in June by the Provisional Constitution and extensively recast in late August and early September. But it was not acting rapidly enough for some impatient members of the thirty-seven (one member had been killed in an automobile accident). In the press there were rumblings of internal dissension, ostensibly with General Madanoğlu and Colonel Türkeş as leaders of two differing factions. Then, on November 13, General Gürsel announced that fourteen members of the Committee were being dropped at the request of the armed forces because their activities "had assumed a character tending to endanger the high interests of the country." [24] He asserted, meaningfully, that the new NUC of twenty-three "would restore the country to a normal democratic way of life"; and a few days later, he told a group of political-science students at Ankara University, "It is impossible to think of a dictatorship in our country." Already, eleven of the fourteen were on their way abroad to serve as civilian attachés on supposedly compulsory two-year appointments.[25]

The leader of these fourteen was Colonel Alparslan Türkeş,[26] a Turk who had come from Cyprus at the age of fifteen. He was a Pan-Turkist and a firm follower of the ideology of Yusuf Akçura. In 1944, he had written some rabid Pan-Turkist poems for which he was imprisoned briefly. Very dynamic and positive in beliefs, speech, and actions, Türkeş had been a principal conspirator and always an outstanding personality. After the coup, he served until September 22 as deputy minister to Gürsel. For a time, observers considered the possibility that Türkeş might oust Gürsel as Nasir had Nagib; indeed, if Gürsel had not "arrested" Türkeş at this moment and "exiled" him to New Delhi, such a turn might well have occurred.

Türkeş and his group differed on many particulars but, in general, were more socialistic than the others and more insistent upon moving ahead rapidly without waiting for all the niceties of democratic action. They were agreed that the NUC should remain in power over an extended period until all reforms were accomplished. This had especially come to light in the debate on a proposed "Law for Unity in National Objectives." NUC deliberations on this proposal were extremely heated and, as Gürsel later admitted, assumed "the aspect of a pitched battle." One need not be surprised, for Türkeş, in an earlier newspaper interview, candidly professed his great heroes to be Tamerlane and Selim I.

With this problem temporarily solved, the reduced NUC proceeded in their work of forming the Second Republic. On January 6, 1961, the Constituent Assembly convened in Ankara in two houses: the Senate, which was composed of the twenty-three of the NUC; and the House of Representatives, which comprised 272 representatives elected or chosen by such groups as political parties, journalists, teachers, labor organizations, judges, university faculties, etc. The job of the Constituent Assembly was to study, debate, amend, and authorize the final draft of the new Constitution, already composed by a special committee of university law professors. Considerable debate ensued; and in March and April, martial law was partially reinstated while Gürsel bluntly warned politicians not to try to revive the dissolved Democrat party under any guise and not to court "former innocent members of that party with their immoral tricks." On May 27, the coup's anniversary, the Constitution was approved by the Assembly and, in the public referendum on July 9, a total of 83 per cent of the eligible voters went to the polls to approve the Constitution, although the ghost of the Democrat party still hovered over Turkish politics, for 38 per cent voted against the Constitution.

Political parties immediately stepped up their activities for the October elections. The Republican People's party under the leadership of Ismet Inönü hoped to win a clear majority and in a sense vindicate the military coup against the Democrats, whose party was now outlawed and disbanded with the trial of their top echelon coming to a close on Yassi Island. Three other parties had prospects of considerable success. The Republican Peasants Nation party, already organized and in existence for several years, was the second pre-coup party to figure in the 1961 elections. Two new parties emerged, each with hope of inheriting the voting strength of the Democrats. The New Turkey party under Akrem Alican sought the support of those intellectuals who had been Democrats in 1950 but who had become genuinely disillusioned with Menderes' politics several years before his fall. The Justice party, which asked unabashedly for the votes of the Democrats, was inaugurated by General Ragib Gümüşpala, a sixty-four-year-old veteran of World War I whom the NUC had first made chief of the general staff and then retired when they reduced the swollen numbers in the top ranks of the military services. The Justice party, even in its name, hinted that they would give justice to the deposed leaders of the former regime.

The electorate went to the polls on October 15 to choose 150 senators and 450 members of the National Assembly. Prior to this, however, there had been a few clashes in the campaigning, and evidence of strong, abiding sympathies for the Democrats had been revealed, especially in rural areas and among the villagers whose influx into Istanbul since World War II radically altered the outlook of that city. The NUC admonished politicians against demagoguery and emotional appeals and acted stringently in a few cases to put teeth into the warning.

On September 15, the trials on Yassi Island came to an end. Fifteen received the death sentence, 31 were given life imprisonment, 418 received prison terms from one to twenty years, 5 had all charges dropped, and 123 were acquitted. Immediately, the NUC commuted 12 of the death sentences, including former President Bayar's, to life imprisonment. The next day, Zorlu and Polatkan, formerly Foreign Minister and Finance Minister respectively, were hanged. Menderes' execution was delayed one day because of his attempted suicide. Without doubt these executions were demanded by the NUC because of anxiety aroused by the specter of possible victory by the Justice party.

The elections were revealing and not too decisive. In the Senate, the division was: Justice party, 70 seats; Republican People's party, 36; New Turkey party, 28; and Republican Peasants Nation party, 16. To

36

these 150 senators were added 15 more appointed by the new President, and also the remaining 22 members of the dissolving NUC (General Madanoğlu had resigned, remarking that he had not engaged in the coup in order to acquire a permanent seat in the Senate). Thus the Senate was to begin with 187 members. In the National Assembly, the count showed: Republican People's party, 173; Justice party, 158; New Turkey party, 65; and Republican Peasants Nation party, 54. As a side light, it may be noted that the Republican People's party polled in the popular vote generally about the same number of votes in 1950, 1954, 1957, and again in 1961. It would seem that there has been a hard core of Republican People's party voters. Moreover, among elected Justice party members of the Assembly were several former Democrats, some prominent, such as Menderes' defense lawyer at the Yassi Island trials, and Melahat Gedik, widow of the last Democrat Minister of Interior.

The lack of a party majority in either house produced two obvious requirements—a coalition government and the necessity of electing Cemal Gürsel President of the Second Republic. The latter was accomplished on October 26 when the two houses in joint session as the Grand National Assembly elevated him to the presidency by a vote of 434 to 173. He resigned promptly from the army and was sworn in.

A coalition government was something different. More than two weeks passed before President Gürsel announced that Ismet Inönü would be Prime Minister, and not until November 20 was Inönü able to form a cabinet, which was finally composed of eleven members from his party and eleven from the Justice party. General Gümüşpala refused to participate, and another Justice party man became Deputy Prime Minister. When it appeared that the Justice party might not co-operate in a coalition, the future of the Second Republic lay in doubt. General Cevdet Sunay, chief of the general staff, returned from Washington to declare the possibility of the army's reassuming its authority if the politicians could not resolve their feuds and allay their personal ambitions. At the same time, it became known that some of the fourteen dismissed members of the NUC and other Turkish radicals were meeting in Paris, perhaps planning a course of action should the newly established government in Turkey stumble before it started.

Are there any lessons to be learned from the recent political events in Turkey? One thing is certain. The military demonstrated by its coup that it is concerned with the progress of Turkey, and as one[27] expressed it, "The May 27th movement was the re-animation of the Atatürk spirit." The military took the rule away from civilians, who were steering a course popular with the conservative, unreformed villagers and small townsmen, and insisted that any civilian group to come to office must pledge to carry Atatürk's reforms to all the nation. Moreover, in its seventeen months of rule, the NUC showed that it was not self-centered when it marked only 24 per cent of the budget for defense and sponsored the first significant efforts in developing a national economic plan for the country by founding, fostering, and protecting the State Planning Office. In addition, it charted a broad program that the military expect of a civilian government and openly demonstrated that a return to military rule would be the result if a civilian regime could not function and get on with the job. The unsuccessful coup of February, 1962, later termed "a mutiny," was a rumbling of younger officers and cadets against the slowness of the civilian regime and the inaction of the İnönü administration in meeting the problems of the day. It was pointed out that in six months of office not a single piece of legislation had been passed.[28] Another important factor in touching off this last "mutiny" was the purging of military extremists, such as Colonel Talât Aydemir, commandant of the Military Academy, by the senior hierarchy of the armed forces in exchange for allowing the politicians to purge some of the extremists of the Justice party.

Another revelation pertains to the place the military holds in Turkish society. Broadly speaking, Turkish officers are among the very best educated persons in Turkey and, therefore, as a class belong to a small elite. Since Turkey is a new state taking the first steps of modernization, the educated elite constitutes a small percentage of the population. Furthermore, this elite firmly believes that the great mass of Turks, mainly villagers, have no conception of the path an evolving Turkish society and state must follow to endure for long. The elite candidly announced that Turkish democracy must be for the people, of the people, and by the elite. Within this small elite, the army comprises a relatively large part. Thus, the military in Turkey does now and will, perhaps for some time to come, exert a deciding influence upon society and government in Turkey.

1. E. A. Speiser, "Cultural Factors in Social Dynamics in the Near East," *Middle East Journal*, VII, No. 2 (Spring, 1953), 133-52; reprinted in S. N. Fisher (ed.), *Social Forces in the Middle East* (Ithaca, N. Y., 1955), pp. 1-22.

2. Paul Wittek, *The Rise of the Ottoman Empire* ("Royal Asiatic Society Monographs," Vol. XXIII [London, 1938]).

3. Albert Howe Lybyer, *The Government of the Ottoman Empire in the Time of Suleiman the Magnificent* ("Harvard Historical Studies," Vol. XVIII [Cambridge, Mass., 1913]).

4. Ernest Edmondson Ramaur, Jr., *The Young Turks: Prelude to the Revolution of 1908* (Princeton, N. J., 1957).

5. Dankwart A. Rustow, "The Army and the Founding of the Turkish Republic," *World Politics*, XI, No. 4 (July, 1959), 513-52.

6. Elaine Diana Smith, *Turkey: Origins of the Kemalist Movement and the Government of the Grand National Assembly (1919-1923)* (Washington, D. C., 1959), pp. 162-72.

7. Uriel Heyd, *Foundations of Turkish Nationalism: The Life and Teachings of Ziya Gökalp* (London, 1950), p. 149.

8. "Turkey's Fresh Start," *Economist* (London), June 4, 1960. pp. 959-61; "The Turkish Takeover," *ibid.*, p. 989; M. Ploumidis, *Turkey following the Revolution* (New York, 1960), pp. 1-3.

9. Bernard Lewis, *The Emergence of Modern Turkey* (London, 1961).

10. Serge A. Zenkovsky, *Pan-Turkism and Islam in Russia* ("Russian Research Center Studies," No. 36 [Cambridge, Mass., 1960]), pp. 38-39, *passim;* Charles Warren Hostler, *Turkism and the Soviets: The Turks of the World and Their Political Objectives* (London, 1957), pp. 143-44, *passim;* and George G. Arnakis, *"Turanism, an Aspect of Turkish Nationalism," Balkan Studies*, I (1960), 19-32.

11. Niyazi Berkes, *Turkish Nationalism and Western Cvilization: Selected Essays of Ziya Gökalp* (New York, 1959).

12. Dankwart A. Rustow, "Politics and Islam in Turkey, 1920-1955," *Islam and the West: Proceedings of the Harvard Summer School Conference on the Middle East, July 25-27, 1955* (The Hague, 1957), p. 81.

13. Personal remark by Walter Livingston Wright, Jr.

14. Necmeddin Sadak in his sociology textbook, published in 1936, quoted in Donald Everett Webster, *The Turkey of Atatürk: Social Process in the Turkish Reformation* (Philadelphia, 1939), p. 165.

15. General Özdilek, quoted in Cevat F. Başkut, Yaşar Kemal, and Ecvet Guresin, *Interviews with Members of Turkey's National Unity Committee* (New York, 1960), p. 45.

16. Lieutenant Colonel S. Karaman, quoted in *ibid.*, p. 124.

17. Colonel Mucip Atakli, quoted in *ibid.*, p. 115.

18. A private letter; see also "Turkish Discontent Boils Over," *Economist* (London), May 7, 1960, pp. 544-45.

19. Ploumidis, *op. cit.*, p. 8.

20. Lieutenant Colonel S. Karaman, quoted in Başkut, Kemal, and Guresin, *op. cit.*, p. 124.

21. General Sitki Ulay, quoted in *ibid.*, p. 34.

22. New York, 1961.

23. "Turkey in the Melting Pot," *Economist* (London), September 3, 1960, pp. 907-8; and "The Captain and the Muezzin," *ibid.*, October 8, 1960, p. 134.

24. *News from Turkey*, Turkish Information Office, New York, XIII, No. 37 (November 15, 1960), and No. 38 (November 23, 1960).

25. "Generals versus Colonels in Turkey," *Economist* (London), November 19, 1960, p. 793.

26. Başkut, Kemal, and Guresin, *op. cit.*, pp. 6-11.

27. Colonel Alparslan Türkeş, quoted in *ibid.*, p. 9.

28. "Angry Young Turks," *Economist* (London), March 3, 1962, pp. 814-15, 818.

The Role of the Military in Iraqi Society
MAJID KHADDURI

IN THE MODERN HISTORY OF THE MIDDLE EAST, Iraq may be regarded as an example par excellence for her experience in a succession of social upheavals, both civil and military. The first military coup d'état occurred more than a quarter of a century ago. Following independence (1932), Iraq has had more than a dozen coups, nine of them carried out by the army, either because leading army officers decided to replace one unpopular civilian government with another or because the army officers desired direct control of authority. Iraq is now governed by the military, and a countercoup is expected to take place at any moment.

The principal changes in government produced by violent means, military or otherwise, since independence were those of 1934, 1936, 1938, 1940-41, 1948, 1952, the abortive coup of 1956, and the Revolution of July, 1958. It is to be noted that these coups have recurred in a cyclical form, each cycle maturing in a two- or four-year period: the coups (tribal or military) before the war recurred in a two-year cycle; those after the war in a four-year cycle.

The first military coup d'état took place in 1936—four years after Iraq had achieved independence. The second coup came in 1938, presumably to re-establish civilian rule, but the army officers continued to control the government from behind the scenes. Five more military coups and countercoups erupted during 1940-41 before civilian rule was re-established.

Since World War II, Iraq has experienced a set of violent changes, beginning in 1948 and attaining a climax in the Revolution of July 14, 1958. Nevertheless, just preceding the latter, a spell of relative tranquility had been enjoyed for seven years. Two reasons had led to the military's withdrawal from politics during that period: the chain of military coups d'état, which culminated in full control of authority by the military during the late 1930's precipitated a conflict with Great Britain over the application of the Anglo-Iraqi Treaty of 1930. This altercation resulted in the collapse of military rule when the army proved unable to face a war with such a foreign power. Later, the existence of foreign forces in the country during World War II discouraged any move that might have been undertaken against the civilian government.

The war, by radio broadcasts and propaganda literature extolling the democratic way of life, aroused political awareness and created an almost universal demand for democratic freedoms. This political consciousness was reflected in the rise of a political "new force" made up of former political parties that had been dissolved and of the new postwar generation that, as subsequent events demonstrated, could be destructive if not permitted to play its role through constitutional channels. One sign of the significance of this political consciousness was the immediate favorable response to the formation of political parties. However, the elder politicians, who may be called the "old oligarchs," reacted violently against the new popular force. Thus, the conflict that ensued between the ruling oligarchs and the "new force" was in the nature of an antagonism between the new generation, which had recently entered the scene of politics and aspired to establish a truly parliamentary government, and the elder politicians, who betrayed authoritarian propensities.

One of the contributing factors that triggered the collapse of the old regime of the oligarchs, not only in Iraq, but in other Arab countries, was the burning question of Palestine. Immediately after the war, there was throughout the Arab world great concern about the future position of Palestine. In Iraq, as indeed in the other Arab countries,

42

the politically conscious public was permitted to express its feelings by street demonstrations, by protests to be sent to foreign powers, and by a free expression in the press, all in the hope that these outbursts might induce Great Britain and the United States to sympathize with nationalist aspirations. The new political parties took an active part in organizing these nationalist activities and demonstrations, a role which helped to strengthen their hold over the people. When the Arab states suffered the loss of their case at the United Nations and defeat in the Palestine war, the people of Iraq joined with the politically conscious populations of other Arab lands in blaming the old oligarchs in power for their mishandling of the Palestine problem and for their failure to impose effective sanctions against Great Britain and the United States. Thus, in the name of Arab rights in Palestine, the new force, represented by political parties and other nationalist organizations, was able, in spite of the strong opposition of the oligarchs, to defy with impunity any group in power that failed in its national duty. Street demonstrations and public disorder became daily affairs which often occurred for reason having nothing to do with national issues.

It was in this atmosphere that the oligarchs, trying to defend themselves against a popular uprising in 1948, were hopelessly defeated. However, the victory of the popular force was short-lived, mainly owing to differences among the leaders of the political parties. Although they had co-operated in their opposition to the elder politicians as well as in overthrowing them from power, the leaders showed a dismal lack of foresight in not providing a positive program of action. Within less than a year, the oligarchs returned to power and the political parties had to learn the lesson of concerted action anew. Within a four-year period, another popular uprising took place, in 1952, and the oligarchs had to face another showdown and national disgrace. But within a year, after a short term of military rule to restore order, they managed to return to power; and the popular force was prompted to stage a third coup four years later, in 1956. This one, however, proved to be abortive. The oligarchs, without concession to popular demands, were determined to suppress the opposition by force, paying no attention to the consequences of their action. These measures exhausted the patience of the army officers, who, having watched the political scene with keen interest, now decided to intervene in order to put an end to the oligarchy.

The popular uprisings, produced in the main by opposition parties and supported by college students and the man in the street, took the form of strikes and street demonstrations. Usually, strikes began suddenly with trifling incidents; but when students and the mob, incited by opposition leaders, rushed to the street, the demonstrations became exceedingly difficult to control. The government, shouted down by familiar slogans, had the alternative of a bloody battle with the mob or resignation. After each successful coup, the new administration tried to learn how to prevent the recurrence of the method used to achieve its coup. When certain tactics became obsolete, resulting in abortive coups, opposition leaders employed new weapons of political opposition. Thus the cycle of eruption continued.

Popular upsurges and street demonstrations, often manifesting the horror of mob psychology, were bound to affect the position of the ruling dynasty itself. In 1948, when the Regent and the King repudiated the action of their own government, the mob shouted, "Long live the King"; but in 1952, when opposition leaders lost confidence in the dynasty, a few of those who took part in the demonstrations shouted, "Down with the monarchy." Anxious to protect the monarchy, the Regent grew frightened and called on the army to restore order. Civilian rule was not re-established before the opposition had been crushed by the armed forces of the state.

The reintroduction of the army into domestic politics, presumably to maintain law and public order, was a very dangerous move. It showed the bankruptcy of civilian rule and tempted a few army officers to play again with the idea of establishing a military government. The story of the Revolution of 1958 has yet to be told, but a word about its origins may be in order.

Early in 1954, a group of young army officers, calling themselves the Free Officers, formed a secret organization. The chief center was in Baghdad, but there were two or three others outside the capital. Their chief preoccupation focused upon enlisting a sufficient number of younger officers, organizing them, and preparing them for the day when a rebellion would be raised.

The greatest obstacle that faced the Free Officers was the lack of

44

ammunition. But this did not keep them from action, for they secretly contacted the Syrian and Egyptian armies, from whom arms were obtained and stored for the day of rebellion against the Iraqi government.

While the Iraqi government denied its officers ammunition, it supplied such to secret organizations in Syria. The Syrian secret groups were working to overthrow their regime and unite Syria with Iraq under the Hashimi dynasty. This move was resented by the Iraqi Free Officers and prompted them to pass on intelligence to the Syrian government that enabled the Syrians to capture the Iraqi arms and punish the Syrian rebel leaders each time arms and armaments were dispatched from Iraq.

No less serious a problem was the timing of the revolution. Several attempts were made which were called off at the last minute because the Free Officers decided that an uprising should never be attempted unless they—the leaders of the army—were sure that they would arrest the ruling triumvirate, the King, the Crown Prince, and General Nuri al-Said. If any one of these were to escape, it was rightly contended, not only could he supply leadership for a countercoup, but the new regime established by the revolution might be overthrown. The opportune moment came on July 14, 1958, when an Iraqi regiment was ordered to proceed to Jordan on the same day the King, the Crown Prince, and General Nuri were to leave Baghdad for Istanbul. Designated to lead this army to Jordan was General Abd al-Karim Qasim, one of the Free Officers, who took advantage of the opportunity and reversed the order: instead of leading the army toward Jordan, he marched on Baghdad. What followed after the revolution, as subsequent developments indicated, was determined more by the chain of events that followed the capture of Baghdad and the liquidation of the monarchy than by a predetermined plan laid down by the Free Officers.

The first fundamental issue that arose was whether Iraq would join the United Arab Republic or remain as a separate political entity. Much has been said about the personal rivalry between Qasim and Arif and the tactical errors committed by Syrian and Egyptian leaders, who expected an easy merging between the new Iraqi regime and the Egypto-Syrian union. The basic obstacle in the way of achieving a union between Iraq and the United Arab Republic, however, was inherent in the rigid constitutional structure of the United Arab Republic. Its unitary nature, which virtually meant that Iraq had to merge with the Egypto-Syrian regime without regard to her internal social structure, rendered the union less capable of attracting Iraq or the other Arab countries. Egypt and Syria, because they are both solidly Sunni by faith and Arabic in language and culture, could perhaps find a common ground for a cohesive national unity;[1] but Iraq is divided, on the one hand, almost half and half into Sunni and Shi'i communities by faith and into Arabs and Kurds—although not evenly in terms of race and language—on the other. A union between Iraq and the United Arab Republic would reduce not only the Shi'a, who claim to constitute the majority of the population of Iraq, to a minority—which had been their unprivileged position under the Ottoman regime—but also the Kurds, already nationally conscious, into a much smaller minority. General Abd al-Karim Qasim, who grasped the significance of these internal factors better than Colonel Arif, stood for Iraqi independence and declared himself against any attempt to join the United Arab Republic. Thus, the centrifugal forces, cleverly manipulated by Qasim, ran contrary to the wishes of the original authors of the Iraqi Revolution.

What happened outwardly after the revolution is well known in terms of bare facts, but the significance of the events lies deeper than what appears on the surface. Looked upon merely in terms of what is achieved negatively, the revolution put an end to the perennial struggle between the old oligarchs, who derived their power mainly from tribalism and feudalism, and the new generation, who sought for a new leadership. It also lifted certain repressive measures and allowed internal social forces, long repressed, to play their role in producing the form of government desired by the people. But this latter situation led to the inevitable ideological conflict between nationalism and communism. Last but not least, the revolution brought the army again into politics and suspended, perhaps indefinitely, civilian rule. Thus, General Qasim's power, although derived in part from his skillful manipulation of competing social forces, is still to a large extent dependent on the army. From such an obviously precarious position, the regime can inspire neither confidence in its ability to maintain public order nor hope for restoring free expression of opinion. At best, Qasim

46

is trying to prevent the outbreak of a civil war between nationalists and communists, both supported by forces let loose in society by the revolution.

The revolution has not yet been able to move into a more constructive stage nor to produce an elite that combines the moderate elements of the existing competing forces. It would be a great calamity if either of the two competing forces should have the upper hand: if the nationalists were to win, the old oligarchs might return to power; and if the communists win, the country would be dominated by the Soviet bloc. No elite has yet emerged to represent the constructive principles of reform either because the revolution has not yet been completed or because it was, from the very beginning, more of a coup d'état than a revolution.

Two fundamental questions, which are closely connected with each other, might now be examined. First, what were the principal objectives of the military in their intervention in politics; and secondly, why did the democratic form of government completely disappear in Iraq?

It is clear from the preceding discussion that the army, like all the other national organizations, was inevitably involved in the struggle between the oligarchs and the new generation. Many of the leading army officers were either directly associated with the ideological groupings or indirectly influenced by them. However, the army officers as a separate group never formulated a set of ideals different from those propounded by other groupings. Instead, they adopted the principal ideas that had already commanded wide appeal among the public and sought to carry them out after they achieved power by force. The army's program, which may be called eclectic since it was borrowed from other groupings, falls into three main categories.

The most significant determination is the wish to establish a modern national state. Not only do the army and other revolutionary leaders advocate this principle, but also moderates and even some of the religious elements. The controversy among the advocates of the traditional Islamic (universal) state is ended, although in theory it is still regarded as the ideal in traditional Islamic society. A modern national state is regarded as the army's ultimate objective, although it is clear to them that none of the Arab states has yet attained that goal fully.

47

The principle of secularism, fully accepted by the Turkish revolutionary leaders, has not yet been formally adopted by Arab leaders, although in practice all Arab military regimes have tacitly approved of it. Secularism has acquired the connotation of separating religion from the state and, perhaps eventually, the disestablishment of Islam. As a result, no Arab revolutionary leader has yet been able to speak frankly on this question, except perhaps Bourguiba (Abu Ruqayba) of Tunisia, who took the bold step in secularizing the law of personal status. The question has been asked: why have the Turkish revolutionary leaders succeeded where Arabs failed? Most contemporary Turkish spokesmen do not regard Islamic law and Islamic institutions as ever having been a part of their national heritage; while to the Arabs, these are regarded as an integral part of their cultural heritage and many of them take such pride in these facets of the national heritage that it is almost mandatory that they be kept and developed. Thus, no serious efforts have been attempted to copy the Turkish experiment of secularization. The prevailing opinion stresses the value of an evolutionary, not a revolutionary, procedure.

Much more serious controversy has been stirred on the question of adopting socialistic measures. It has been the Arab rather than Turkish thinkers who have been tempted to introduce socialism into the Muslim society. One may wonder why the Arabs, having refused to trade Islam for other modes of loyalties, should toy with the idea of adopting socialistic principles. Although certain Islamic principles are incompatible wih socialistic doctrines (such as the abolition of property rights and the materialistic view of life), other tenets are not opposed to socialism. Muslim socialists argue that Islam does not tolerate the great disparity between rich and poor and that Islam is inherently opposed to exploitation and poverty. They maintain that Islam imposes the obligation upon the community as a whole to regulate its economic life on an equitable basis. Thus, socialism in Arab lands is justified on religious grounds. Although they have separated religion from the state, the Turks, for political considerations, have consciously opposed the infiltration of socialist philosophies and have tried to find the answer to their economic problems in a mixture of free enterprise and statism.

To the question, can the Arabs experiment with ideas borrowed from socialist regimes without losing their own cultural identity, the answer has invariably been given that socialistic principles may be regarded as a corrective to existing social maladies, and that their adoption, together with ideas from the West, is a healthy approach to social reform. This argument may be justified on the ground that the history of Islam demonstrates that the Arabs have been capable of blending foreign elements of culture and creating their own synthesis. Thus, if the Arabs could absorb ideas and institutions from both West and East in order to create institutions adapted to Arab needs, the experiment might well be worth attempting, since by past experience the Arabs have been frustrated in transplanting foreign institutions which were not adapted to particular Arab needs. If a synthesis of foreign ideas and institutions emerges, the Arab countries might be saved from domination by any one type of ideology. The danger in this kind of thinking is that the Arab reformer might succumb to the influx of radical leftist ideas before he had the time to effect such a synthesis.

Closely related to the rise of military rule is the question of why the democratic regime in Iraq (and the other Arab countries) collapsed, thereby leaving an opening to the army to intervene. The answer is by no means easy, but an analysis of the operation of democratic government may be of help in finding an answer.

To begin with, parliamentary government was a novel form of government which the Iraqi people, for centuries accustomed to authoritarian rule, were neither familiar with nor appreciative of its complicated processes. It is true that the Arabs, whether in Iraq or in other Arab lands, have enjoyed a certain form of social democracy, but political democracy (in the form of parliamentary government) ran contrary to traditional systems in which the ruler, though he listened to opposing opinions, made his final decision irrespective of the advice of counsellors. Moreover, the Islamic religion, though opposed in principle to absolute rule, has tolerated authoritarian rulers on the ground that despotism was preferable to anarchy and instability.

Following World War I when Iraq was placed under the mandate against the desire of the politically conscious public, the ruling class (composed of nationalists who co-operated with the Western Powers) accepted the democratic form of government without trying to adapt it to existing conditions. Parliamentary government worked to the satisfaction of the nationalists, since they used it as a forum to oppose mandatory control. When the mandate was terminated, parliamentary life began to appear as meaningless: the elder nationalists (the oligarchs), who inherited authority from the mandatory power (Britain), showed little respect for parliamentary control and began to betray traditional authoritarian tendencies. The new generation, which grew up in the interim period and became active in politics after World War II, began to discover how scandalously the democratic processes could be misused, and advocated the re-establishment of a truly parliamentary system in which the younger men could take an active part. The oligarchs resisted and tried to suppress the movement by force. This conflict between the oligarchs and the new generation is in the last analysis the cause of the coups and the countercoups that have been taking place in Iraq during the past two decades.

Experience in the other Arab states has shown that such a conflict usually resolves itself by the collapse of parliamentary government and the installation of a military dictatorship. Iraq, it will be recalled, has had her own experiments in military dictatorships; but such experiments proved to be short-lived. Iraq's greatest asset militating against permanent dictatorships, civil or military, is her complex social structure. The almost equal division of Iraq into two Muslim sects, on the one hand, and into two ethnic communities (to say nothing about the existence of numerous smaller communities) on the other, has resulted in the operation of a check-and-balance system against any dictatorship deriving its support from one community. None has survived for very long. As a result, perhaps no form of government other than that in which all the communities can be represented will fit Iraqi society; such a form is the parliamentary type of democracy. But parliamentary government in Iraq has been discredited because it was not immune to corruption and exploitation. It was, however, not the fault of parliamentary government that many sins were committed in its name; if it failed to operate to the satisfaction of the people, it failed because it was transplanted into a society entirely unprepared for it.

The division of Iraqi society into various communities is only a negative factor, since it provides merely a check against dictatorship, not a positive factor for promoting a truly parliamentary form of government. Governments, like other social institutions, must develop

50

by a slow and steady process. Iraq may well experience more social upheaval before she discovers the form of democratic government that fits her social structure.[2]

1. Even in the case of Syrian-Egyptian merging, the unitary form of union proved impractical in holding the two parties together. There were, to be sure, other causes for the collapse of the experiment.

2. The writer has drawn freely from his article "The Role of the Military in Middle East Politics," *American Political Science Review*, XLVII (1953), 511-24, reprinted with some changes as "The Army Officer: His Role in Middle Eastern Politics" in *Social Forces in the Middle East*, ed. Sydney Nettleton Fisher (Ithaca, N. Y., 1955), pp. 162-83; and from his book *Independent Iraq* (London, 1960).

The Role of the Military in Society and Government in Syria and the Formation of the U.A.R.

GORDON H. TORREY

THE REAR-VIEW APPROACH that history gives to the problems of the present has been termed a praiseworthy one, but too much dependence on the past may blind one to the future. Syria, in the light of her recent revolt and breaking away from her union with Egypt, may be a case in point. Nevertheless, an examination of the interplay between politicians and the military prior to that union is both timely and instructive.

Syria during the years 1949-53 underwent five coups d'état, twenty-one cabinets, two military dictatorships, and one war. No other country in the Middle East, with the exception of Iraq, has had such a turbulent history in as short a time. Yet Syria survives and undoubtedly will play an important role in the days ahead. Because of her geographical position, conflicting ties with other Arab states, and rival political factions, which have failed to submerge their differences for the good of the nation, Syria is likely to be the pivotal area of the Middle East in the foreseeable future. Syrian nationalism, communism, socialism, capitalism, religious sectarianism, and Nasirism, all meet here to struggle for supremacy.

53

Military intervention in civilian politics in the Middle East usually has been motivated by one of three basic reasons: to satisfy the desire for power for its own sake; to carry out reformist or revolutionary programs which the military believes have been thwarted by incompetent or reactionary civilian politicians; or to protect what the army believes to be its vital interests. Intervention by the Syrian military in the country's politics largely has been for the latter two reasons.

Za'im's coup in March, 1949, stemmed from what the officer corps thought was calculated defamation of the army by the politicians in an attempt to save their own skins after the Palestine debacle, as well as to stave off large reductions in army strength and appropriations. The Shishakli coup against Hinnawi the same year was motivated largely by political considerations: the fear that Iraqi-Syrian relations were reaching the point where Syria might be swallowed up in a Hashimite-ruled monarchy with the Syrian army's identity and position downgraded. In neither of these coups were socio-ideological considerations predominant and in each case there was co-operation between certain political elements and army conspirators. In the years 1954-58, ideological principles came to dominate the political arena and the methods of, and causes for, military intervention differed sharply from those that had gone before.

Evolving from the Troupes Spéciales, an internal security force used by the French authorities to keep order during the mandate, the small, 5,000-man Syrian army was led in 1946 by men who had been Ottoman or French trained. It consisted of volunteers and included many men from the Syrian minorities: Armenians, Kurds, Circassians, etc. This force, while there was a majority of Syrian officers, always had Frenchmen in the higher ranks and remained under French control until the end of the mandate. Following Syrian independence, the army was increased, but it was still a small force at the time of the Palestine War of 1948.

Mirroring the Syrian social structure much more closely than did the Egyptian army that of Egypt, the Syrian army was a combined volunteer-conscript force. In its early years, leadership came largely from the upper echelons of Syrian society and in many ways was connected with the country's "fifty families." Atasi, Mardam, Nizam al-Din, and numerous others were names on the army rosters, as well

54

as those encountered in parliament. However, unlike Iraq, the Syrian army was not looked upon as a springboard to political office and, hence, was not considered suitably attractive for many representatives of the oligarchical families; better opportunities lay in the fields of law, medicine, trade, and estate management from whence political careers could be based. This was especially so after independence.

However, the army did offer opportunities for prestige and advancement, as well as a comfortable life, for sons of middle- and lower-class families. A study of the backgrounds of a number of prominent younger officers revealed that most came, not from the two major cities, but from the provinces and smaller towns. Homs and Hama were more often the places of birth than Damascus and Aleppo. Likewise, many candidates for the Homs Military Academy were drawn from middle-class families—those of small landholders, merchants, and even blacksmiths—who were the products of the rapidly expanding educational system. These men had little in common with the nation's traditional rulers and many came to be imbued with Pan-Arab nationalistic and socialist ideals. While more concerned with the peacetime amenities of army life than with careers as professional soldiers, the Syrian officer corps soon came to be highly critical of the manner in which the country's civilian leaders fumbled and fought among themselves for their own selfish ends. This is not to say that all officers had a sense of mission; rivalries for position and influence were just as prevalent in the army as in the political arena.

An additional factor affecting the outlook of that portion of the officer corps that came to be influential after 1954 was its indoctrination in the public schools and at the Homs Military Academy. During the mandate period, Syrian students were deliberately made politically conscious, trained in political agitation, and imbued with the natural right and need of student participation in politics by the country's nationalist leaders. Student strikes were utilized as a means of expressing dissatisfaction with the French occupation. Thus, when public-school graduates reached the academy, they were already inculcated with the desirability of political agitation and were receptive to further political indoctrination. At the academy, many in the classes of 1947-48 were ideologically influenced by Colonel Jamal Faysal, one of their instructors. Faysal was a strong Pan-Arabist whose views closely

55

paralleled those of what came to be the Ba'th party and of Egypt's Gamal Abd al-Nasir. This group of officers, which came to be termed the "Little Revolutionary Command Council" (RCC) because of its similarity to the Nasir-led group in Egypt, believed ardently in Arab unity, social revolution, and the ousting of Western influences. They also realized the efficacy of co-operation with like-minded civilian elements and the important role that the army could play as a social and political force in carrying out their aspirations.

Likewise, knowing that the country's traditional leadership found it difficult, if not impossible, to move with the times and to bring about necessary social and economic changes, this group, as well as younger civilian political aspirants, saw that the only solution lay in such drastic methods as military intervention in the government, or coups d'état, if necessary. With this background in mind, it is of interest to view the role of the Syrian army in politics and how it evenutally led to the formation of the United Arab Republic in February, 1958.

Muhammad Jinnah once said, "It is easier to go to jail and fight for freedom than to run a government." This proved to be the case in Syria after independence. The years 1946-49 were characterized by a rapid disorganization and deterioration of the governmental processes. The dominant Nationalist party regime used its control of the government for purposes of personal aggrandizement, nepotism, and corruption on a whole-sale scale. Constitutional guarantees were disregarded, governmental critics arrested, newspapers suppressed, and political opponents crushed. Constitutional procedures were ignored or contravened, laws passed without a parliamentary quorum, auditing of expenditures obfuscated, opposition members of parliament surveilled, and laws unenforced.

The Nationalists lost their hold on the government in the 1947 elections, but this did not bring the country new leadership, only a different set of politicians. It looked as if the country was to continue under the ministrations of its incompetent and avaricious political mentors until conditions became unbearable and a popular revulsion resulted in a social upheaval.

Although almost none could envision it at the time, the country was soon fated to pass over a watershed—the Palestine War of 1948. Syrian public opinion was at a feverish pitch against the creation of a

Jewish state in Palestine, and all Syrians were confident that forceful Arab action could prevent the partition. When Syrian volunteers entered Palestine bent on crushing Israel, many politicians flocked to join units in the hope of becoming heroes overnight. Syrian optimism knew no bounds and public opinion, aided and abetted by the country's political leaders, clung to the myth of Arab military superiority. As the vision of quick victory receded, criticism of the government rapidly increased.

The disastrous Palestine campaign and economic troubles, accompanied by widespread rumors of governmental corruption in the war effort, brought on an epidemic of strikes and demonstrations. By November, 1948, clashes between pro- and anti-government supporters reduced the country to a state of near anarchy. The Mardam cabinet resigned and the country was without a government. It lacked competent leadership, was possessed of a turbulent and distressed citizenry, was subject to a collapsing economy, and burdened with an army that felt betrayed by a coterie of scheming politicians. Surely this was the moment for a Boulanger or a Napoleon to appear on the scene. One did in the person of Colonel Husni al-Za'im, commander in chief of the army. Za'im ordered the army to intervene, imposed martial law, restored order and formed a new cabinet. These bold measures catapulted him into national prominence.

Mardam's cabinet was succeeded by one headed by Khalid al-Azm, a clever man without convictions but great ambitions. The tenor of the time was echoed by one Damascus paper which declared that if Azm's cabinet failed, the country would be left to the mobs instead of the statesmen. When Azm attempted to cut army expenditures and reduce its strength, and, after a special tribunal to investigate corruption, picked an army officer as its first accused, the army believed this to be a ruse whereby the politicians were attempting to shift the blame for the Palestine fiasco onto the army's shoulders.

A "Note of Protest," which Za'im, in the army's name, sent to President Quwatli in late March, 1949, was turned aside by the President with the remark that the officers were acting like "village headmen" in presenting petitions. A further warning was ignored and, succumbing to pressure from younger officers, Za'im struck on March 30 and overthrew the Quwatli-Azm regime. Za'im then attempted the formation of a provisional government which would include political leaders. None offered their services—although a few agreed to give tacit support—despite Za'im's threat to dissolve parliament if they refused. The exception was Akram al-Hawrani, who, in all probability, had been made privy to Za'im's plans to carry out the coup.

Za'im was a graduate of the Ottoman Military Academy at Constantinople, had served in the Troupes Spéciales, and was an extremely ambitious and unscrupulous officer. He had no particular social gospel to induce him to overthrow the established order, and his basic motive was to protect the army's interests. However, short as his reign was, he did initiate a number of reforms which left a lasting imprint: the abolition of hereditary *waqfs* (pious trusts), a new civil code, and plans for distribution of public lands to peasants. He was a reformer, not a revolutionary.

Za'im's failure to carry out radical social reforms irritated Hawrani, a man who believed that the Syrian social order had be revolutionized; his anti-Iraqi policy antagonized the Populist party and pro-Hashimites; and his violation of the spirit of Arab hospitality in the Sa'da affair lost him much public support. Za'im's delusions of grandeur and assumption of the airs of a caesar, rather than those of the head of a republican state, made him a laughing stock. Often he modestly compared himself to Atatürk and Napoleon and on one occasion is reputed to have declared, "I am the grand seigneur, I am King." However, he might have survived had he not aroused the ire of his own officer class when he imprisoned and dismissed former military supporters. Four and a half months after he had seized power, Za'im was overthrown and assassinated by an army group led by Colonel Hinnawi.

Like his predecessor, Muhammad Sami al-Hinnawi was Ottoman-trained. In contrast to Za'im, he advocated a pro-Iraqi policy. Hinnawi damned Za'im for creating a situation where people "disparaged the army" and ended his communique with what came to be standard phrasing in all coups—that the army had saved the nation from tyranny and now would retire to its barracks. Thus, Za'im was not condemned for carrying out the first coup, but for betraying it. The Za'im coup was meant to sweep away the old corrupt leadership and instal a new civilian group to guide the nation along a wise path.

Rather than pick up the pieces and restore the *ancien régime*, a constitutional assembly was elected which laid the foundations for a new state. The Nationalists boycotted the elections and thereby excluded themselves from the legislative process that evolved when the constituent assembly transformed itself into a parliament in 1950.

Meanwhile, Hinnawi was deposed in mid-December because his pro-Iraqi sympathies alarmed anti-Iraqi army elements led by Colonel Adib Shishakli, who declared that the army had no intention of inter-fering in politics, "unless necessary." A new cabinet was formed by Azm, who now was satisfactory to the army and the anti-Iraqi politicians. Akram al-Hawrani, a boyhood friend of Shishakli, served as the link between the two groups, and became Minister of Defense to watch over the army's interests. Later in the year, Hawrani was replaced by Colonel Fawzi Silu in an open display of army influence.

Until December, 1951, there was an uneven contest between the anti-army Populists and the Shishakli-Hawrani bloc. This ended on November 29, 1951, when Shishakli openly seized the reins of govern-ment and ousted a Populist cabinet after Prime Minister Dawalibi had assumed the defense portfolio and a threat to retire Shishakli was in the offing. President Atasi resigned three days later and Parliament was dissolved. Colonel Silu was made Chief of State, but Shishakli re-mained Chief of the Military Council.

Shishakli was pro-Western, a Syrian Social National party sympa-thizer, and had broken with Za'im over the Sa'da affair. The Shi-shakli coup was similar to those that had gone before in that he soon attempted to return civilian affairs to the politicians, but with strings attached. First, he sought Nationalist participation in the government, dangling suppression of the Populists as bait, but the Nationalists re-fused. Co-operation with Hawrani continued until the next spring when a falling-out occurred over the slow progress and moderation of Shishakli's social policies. Until his downfall, Hawrani continued to attempt to entice the politicians to work with him, but failed.

In time, Shishakli was pushed from the position of a behind-the-scenes manipulator into the role of the leader of the state. Backed by only a handful of military supporters, he lacked a dedicated body of civilian followers. Although he did institute a number of modest re-forms—increased income taxes, credit facilities for the peasants, and plans to improve Latakia harbor and to drain the al-Ghab swamp—

they were insufficient to win him the support of leftists and the middle class, while even these mild measures were opposed by conservative elements. The creation of his own political party, the Arab Liberation Movement, failed to win public support for his regime; and a punitive campaign against the Druze at the end of 1953 antagonized a considerable part of the army leadership. Following student demonstrations sparked by Hawrani and the country's traditional political leaders, Shishakli was ousted at the end of February, 1955.

Neither Za'im, Hinnawi, nor Shishakli could be termed social revolutionaries or vigorous advocates of a unified Arab state. During their era, however, among the younger officers, a new school of thought was growing that paralleled the thinking in some civilian quarters. These officers believed in social revolution, Arab unity, and anti-Westernism; all had been humiliated by the birth of Israel; and they took great encouragement from Nasir's victory over King Faruq and the politicians in Egypt. Some were Ba'thist and others were not. The most notable among these younger officers was Abd al-Hamid Sarraj.

Sarraj came from a well-to-do Hama family and had graduated from the Homs Academy in what came to be the famous class of 1947. After the Za'im coup, Sarraj was appointed Za'im's aide-de-camp, and during Shishakli's regime became chief of army intelligence. Personally honest, courageous, and intelligent, the ambitious Sarraj quickly exploited his position to create an extremely efficient intelligence organization. By 1956, his civilian and military intelligence apparatus extended into all parts of the country at all levels and made him the strongest figure in Syria. Although never a member of the Ba'th, Sarraj co-operated closely with it until the union with Egypt when he then sided with Nasir against the party. A believer in Pan-Arab ideals and in social revolution, he was, until he resigned when removed from his Syrian locus of power to Cairo, Nasir's faithful proconsul in Syria after the formation of the United Arab Republic. Sarraj played the role of a guardian of what he believed to be Syrian and Arab nationalist interests, not that of a leader; and he never attempted to build up a political following. His ideological convictions appear to be rather vague.

Another contemporary who came to be active in army politics along with Sarraj was Lieutenant Colonel Amin al-Nafuri. A native of Nabak, a village between Damascus and Homs, Nafuri served as an enlisted man before graduating from the military academy and rose rapidly until he commanded the armored battalion in 1949. By early 1957, he had risen to deputy chief of staff. He was not a Ba'thist, but had gained the support of many junior officers and men of peasant origin, many of whom resented the dominance of the Sarraj "city-men" group in army politics. Nafuri was a more popular leader than Sarraj, probably because of his former enlisted man's status. As far as can be ascertained, Nafuri adhered to no particular ideology, but was an ambitious and competent officer who played army politics purely to get ahead.

An officer of quite a different philosophy was Afif al-Bizri, who became Syria's communist chief of staff in 1957. Born in Lebanon in 1914, he served on the Israeli-Syrian Mixed Armistice Commission in 1948-49. In 1950, Bizri was sent to France for training in the French Army Geographical School, where he remained until 1953. At this time, he was presumed to be pro-Iraqi, but his communist connections may have been acquired during this stay in France. Following the assassination of Deputy Chief of Staff Malki in 1955, Bizri was appointed president of the military tribunal that tried the alleged assassins, members of the Syrian Social National party. He became army chief of personnel in 1957; by August of the same year, he was promoted to the rank of major-general and made chief of staff. Strangely enough, his career was furthered by his connections with the Ba'th and Nafuri. He, too, had a following that made him a force to be reckoned with in army political maneuverings.

From 1946 to 1949, parliamentary democracy was tried and found wanting. During the period 1949-54, military dictatorship also failed to give the country the leadership it required. In 1954, Syria entered a new era in which certain military and civilian elements co-operated in attempts to control the nation.

Following the anti-Shishakli coup, some army officers—notably Sarraj, a former Shishakli supporter, and Ba'th partisan Captain Mustafa Hamdun—soon began to fear that the army was losing prestige by its withdrawal from the political scene and that the police and gendarmerie would be returned to civilian control. Sarraj and Hamdun are said to have protested "civilian interference" and threatened a coup. Failing to secure army support for such a venture, they gave up their plans for a coup, but successfully resisted assignments abroad as military attachés, a move which would have removed them from Syrian political affairs. Despite the transfer of the gendarmerie to the interior ministry in late March, 1954, army influence in the government remained so strong that the defense minister had difficulty exerting civilian control over the military establishment. Throughout the remainder of the year, there were continual rumors that the army was attempting to pull the strings from behind the scene, but the September, 1954, elections appeared to belie such allegations.

The greatest election surprise was the pulling power of the Ba'th, whose bloc in the parliament now numbered 22 seats out of the 142, a threefold increase from the 1950 parliament. The Ba'th was by far the most cohesive and disciplined group, and its weight was felt in disproportionate amount to its size. It had profited from growing anti-Westernism and general disgust with the older parties. The 1954 elections signified the end of Syria's traditional political forces and their replacement by the left-wing of the Arab nationalist movement. The new parliament was weak, inseparably divided, and utterly lacking in direction and leadership. It was easy prey for a well-organized minority, such as the Ba'th and its army allies.

Foreign relations were fated to become the most controversial question in Syrian politics during the years 1955-56. Relations with Iraq and Jordan improved, while strains appeared in the Cairo-Damascus axis after Shishakli's fall. The prospect of Iraqi adherence to the Turko-Pakistani Pact in 1955 alarmed Nasir and his attempts to draw Syria back into the Egyptian orbit involved him in Syrian internal politics. The struggle between the pro-Iraqi and pro-Nasir political and army factions dominated Syrian affiairs and led to such strange temporary alliances as the Ba'th with the Populists and the bloc led by Khalid al-Azm with the Ba'th. Cabinets came and went, victims of various pressures from politicians and the army. Finally, in February, 1955, after army pressure, left-wing Nationalist Sabri al-Asali formed a cabinet that definitely came out on Egypt's side. The Nationalists had decided to bow to the army's will in order to stay in power until the presidential elections. The Populists, as divided as the Nationalists, temporarily acquiesced. The Saudis, Egyptians, the Ba'th, and the pro-Egyptian army faction began to exert strong pressure for the signing of an Egyptian-Syrian alliance.

The assassination of Deputy Chief of Staff Colonel Adnan al-Malki on April 22, 1955, ushered in a new type of leftist army officer, and Ba'thist co-operation now aimed at relentlessly destroying all rightist opposition. Taking a page from the Communists, Ba'thist partisans within and without the army methodically discredited their opponents by means of a series of "treason trials" that left the mass of Syrian politicians cowed. Seizing on the fact that Malki's assassin was a member of the Syrian Social National party, the army carried out a purge trial that broke the back of the party in Syria and resulted in the execution of two members and the imprisonment of many others. In order to excuse their extra-legal arrest and trial of civilians, the leftists dragged out the bogeyman of an "imperialist plot," which the SSNP had allegedly planned with United States backing. The defense was intimidated and the arrested tortured. President Atasi could only protest the illegal actions, which were aided and abetted by leftwing Nationalist Prime Minister Sabri al-Asali and his Ba'thist allies. Army-cabinet co-operation was so close by now that Asali often held cabinet meetings at his or at Foreign Minister Azm's home so that Chief of Staff Shuqayr could attend.

Shuqayr's co-operation with the leftist army faction prompted a group of conservative officers to plan a coup which would remove the chief of staff and oust Ba'thist officers. However, in mid-July, 1955, the key members of the conspiracy were arrested. This now left control of the army largely in the hands of Shuqayr and three junior officers; G-1 Colonel Jamal Faysal, G-2 Captain Abd al-Hamid Sarraj, and Captain Ahmad al-Hunaydi, commander of an armored battalion at Qatana. Sarraj and Hunaydi had been classmates at the military academy and were the leaders of numerous Ba'thist-inclined officers who looked to Faysal, their former instructor, as their mentor.

Although leftist officers apparently favored Khalid al-Azm over Shukri al-Quwatli in the 1955 presidential election, the army adopted a "hands-off" posture, probably due to divisions within the officer corps. In any case, Quwatli was a satisfactory second choice, since he was pro-Egyptian and was thought to be susceptible to pressure.

The drift toward the left, which started in 1954, picked up momentum in the fall of 1955, and the Ba'th and Communists rapidly gained adherents. This was given impetus by discrediting the conservative leadership, by the creation of a pro-Soviet attitude with a concomitant vilification of the West, and by the Ba'th's preaching of Arab unity. The Ba'th and its sympathizers came to be ensconced in important positions in the army and throughout the government, as well as among the press and students. The arms deal with Czechoslovakia, pushed by the leftists, was concluded at this time, and the Syrian-Egyptian Defense Pact was signed almost simultaneously. Both increased the prestige of the Communists and Ba'th. By early 1956, many conservative politicians thought it futile to oppose the leftward drift.

A maneuver by which the Populists evidently thought they would win the army's gratitude was their proposal of a "National Pact" to which all parties would subscribe. This included enunciation of a neutralist foreign policy and the strengthening of the army. However, this merely whetted the military's appetite for increased influence in the government on national-defense grounds. Only the Ba'th and its army allies profited by the pact, which called for the formation of a "national" cabinet and bound it to the pact's goals. Hawrani's prestige was increased and opportunistic politicians flocked to get on the Ba'th bandwagon. The "national" cabinet was formed by Asali in mid-June, 1956, and the Ba'th secured two choice portfolios: foreign affairs and national economy.

Meanwhile, the Ba'th pushed through the creation of a parliamentary committee to negotiate federal union with Egypt. However, remembering his rebuff when he had promoted Egyptian-Sudanese union, Nasir stalled and suggested "further talks."

Finally, in July, 1956, Chief of Staff Shuqayr was forced out by a combination of Ba'thist and rightist army and civilian elements and a faction of the "Little RCC," which included Colonel Nafuri and Shuqayr's deputy, the conservative Colonel Nizam al-Din, who stepped into Shuqayr's post. The Ba'th and Sarraj were infuriated, since they had assisted in the ouster in the expectation that Sarraj would succeed him. This and Nasir's heel-dragging regarding union with Egypt gave a boost to conservative morale which was to be short-lived.

The 1956 Suez War doomed any possibility that the traditional forces could stave off the rapidly increasing swing to the left. Pro-Western elements were brought into disrepute, despite the stand of the United

States, and the country was drowned in a tide of pro-Nasir and pro-Soviet sentiment. Ba'thist and communist popularity skyrocketed.

Operating under martial law imposed at the time of the Israeli attack, Sarraj "discovered" an Iraqi plot to overthrow the regime. *Mirabile dictu,* Damascus Radio accused Iraq of smuggling arms into Syria for a coup supported by the British, French, Turks, and Israelis. Forty-seven anti-leftist politicians and army officers were among the accused, including six former ministers and several deputies belonging to the Populist and Nationalist parties. In March, 1957, following trial in a "kangeroo military court," presided over by a crypto-Communist, twelve death sentences, including one for the son of ex-President Atasi, and long sentences for all but six of the defendants were handed down. The unprecedented harshness of the sentences was intended to terrorize any further conservative opposition.

With many of their opponents in jail and others terrorized, Hawrani and Azm emasculated the regular political parties by pressing a "parliamentary pledge" through parliament whereby all deputies would forego "partisan" interests. The Asali cabinet was reorganized and the army's protege Khalid al-Azm became defense minister.

The first half of 1957 was characterized by rapidly changing alliances and rivalries amongst the politicians and army officers. March saw Azm siding with the rightists against Sarraj, as was Nafuri's group. However, when the Ba'th secured control of the armored units at Qatana, Azm switched his support to the left. The army now was split into three factions; those of Sarraj, Nafuri, and a neutral group of officers called the Damascenes, led by Colonel Daghistani. This last group attempted to exile Sarraj to Cairo as military attaché but failed. No faction was sufficiently powerful to press through its desires. A mid-May attempt by the Damascenes to unseat Sarraj and transfer his and Nafuri's supporters to the U.S.S.R. on training assignments only partially succeeded This brought about a tactical alliance between Sarraj, Nafuri, and Akram al-Hawrani and the subsequent promotion of Sarraj supporters over the heads of senior officers.

August's "American plot" was utilized by the leftists to oust the remaining rightist officers in responsible army and police positions. At the same time, a purge of "imperialist lackeys" in the government was engineered by Hawrani. So far, the Ba'th, its army allies, and the

Communists had co-operated successfully in crushing the conservative opposition, and in bringing the country into the Nasir and Soviet Bloc camps, whose interests happened to coincide at the time. The next phase was to be the struggle between the pro-Nasir and communist factions for control of the country.

Chief of Staff Nizam al-Din fell in the aftermath of the "American plot" and Communist Colonel Afif al-Bizri replaced him, while Nafuri became Bizri's deputy. Nafuri was now identified with the pro-Soviet clique; five months before, he had been working with rightist elements. Bizri's brother, Salih, was commander of the Popular Resistance Organization, which numbered in the neighborhood of 100,000 armed civilians, many of them Communist. Further setting the stage for what might appear as a Soviet takeover was the conclusion by Azm of a $140-million development loan. It appeared to many that Syria might soon become a communist satellite. The Ba'th was seriously alarmed at this prospect and Nasir, after a hurried visit from Quwatli, also became concerned; both envisioned an Azm-Bizri seizure of power. The Ba'th now realized that it had been used by the Communists, rather than using them. It now sought political allies; however, the Populists rejected an overture by Hawrani for co-operation, although rightist support did win him the influential speakership of parliament, but no Ba'th-conservative working alliance ensued.

The prospect of municipal elections, scheduled for November, heightened Ba'thist fears. With the Communists running as many candidates as the Ba'th itself and the army commanded by Bizri, the Ba'th could envision widespread communist gains on the local government level which could lead to an undermining of the Ba'thist position throughout the country. The general elections, due in September, 1958, could be a disaster! Therefore, the Ba'th used all possible influence to have the elections delayed. Since this suited Populist and other conservative leaders, the government indefinitely postponed the balloting, despite objections from Azm and the Communists. Having won this delaying action, the now panicky Ba'th felt the only way out was union with Egypt.

Attempting to counter the Ba'thist campaign for union with Egypt, Azm sought to build up a civilian counterpart to his army backing by the formation of a "Progressive Party," which was to be a front for the Communists and other opponents of union. This maneuver gave pro-unionists a further sense of urgency; and in mid-January, a military and political mission suddenly flew to Cairo. This development took Nasir unawares and his reluctance to carry out a precipitous union was only overcome when the Syrian leaders agreed to complete unity, not federal union as hitherto had been envisioned. Uncertain of their ability to avert a communist seizure of power, the Syrians felt they had no other choice.

Following the union of the two states in February, a number of politically active Syrian military leaders exchanged their uniforms for civilian suits and became ministers in the combined United Arab Republic cabinet formed on March 6, 1958. Likewise, several of Syria's leftist political leaders also were included in the new ruling organ. Abd al-Hamid Sarraj became Nasir's proconsul in Syria with the title of Minister of Interior for the Syrian Region; Mustafa Hamdun occupied the post of Minister of Social Affairs for the Syrian Region; Ahmad Abd al-Karim, another colonel, guided Municipal and Rural Affairs with the title of minister; and Amin al-Nafuri took over the Syrian Communications Ministry. Ba'thists Akram al-Hawrani and Salah al-Din Bitar occupied the posts of vice president of the U.A.R. and Minister of State, respectively. National party leader Sabri al-Asali, too, was made a vice president. Jamal Faysal was appointed commander of the U.A.R. First Army, the old Syrian army. While elevating the officers on the political scene, Nasir, at the same time, safely removed most potential threats from command positions in the army.

Gradually, as the union continued and cabinet reorganizations were carried out, several of the early advocates, both leftist civilian and military, for union of Syria and Egypt dropped out of participation in the government and were replaced by apolitical personalities. Vice-President Sabri al-Asali was the first to resign, in October, 1958. A year later, Nasir accepted the resignations of such former pro-union stalwarts as Vice-President Hawrani, Salah al-Din Bitar—both Ba'thists—and the ex-officers Abd al-Ghani Qannut and Mustafa Hamdun; May, 1960, saw Nafuri's departure. Hawrani and Bitar's resignations were an expression of disillusionment with the union, especially their disappointment over Nasir's refusal to allow the Ba'th to assume the role of the sole U.A.R. political party.

A cabinet reshuffle in March, 1960, brought several more politically conscious officers into civilian positions: Colonel Akram Dayri took over the Ministry of Labor and Social Affairs; Colonel Ahmad Hunaydi came to preside over the Ministry of Agarian Reform; and Colonel Jamal al-Sufi the Ministry of Supply. By early 1960, Sarraj had been elevated to the presidency of the Syrian Executive Council. Just before the beginning of 1961, another military man, Colonel Tuma Awadat Allah, was brought into the cabinet as Minister of Municipal and Rural Affairs.

As economic and political strains in the union increased during 1961, Nasir tightened the controls over Syria and installed Sarraj in a position in Cairo, possibly fearing that the Syrian strong man might capitalize on the unrest there to lead a secession movement. Finding his Cairo office a sinecure rather than a responsible position, Sarraj resigned and returned to Syria. This may have been one of Nasir's rare cases of political misjudgment; removing the ubiquitous Sarraj from his Syrian locale may have been just the break that dissident Syrian army officers needed to plot the September 28, 1961, revolt which sundered the United Arab Republic.

In conclusion, some general observations may be made regarding military intervention in the political affairs of Syria. The Za'im and Hinnawi regimes were too short-lived to make any lasting impact on economic and social conditions. While the Shishakli's tenure was over four years, it lacked both the will and the ability to carry out social revolution. In the post-Shishakli period, internal political maneuvering for power occupied so much of the various governments' energies that social reform largely fell into the background. Also, the social revolutionaries did not dominate the scene until shortly prior to the union with Egypt. However, the 1957 Syro-Soviet development loan was an indication of what they had in mind—to develop the country's economic potential by means of state enterprise.

The Syrian army, in a sense, has served as the arbiter of power and, in all probability, has had more public support than any other single group in the country. It does not operate in a vacuum but is a reflection of the different social strata, their cliques, and groupings. However, there are inherent difficulties in delving into this problem; political relationships, family ties, educational backgrounds, and the like concerning many individuals are unavailable. At the present time, the army appears to be serving as a safety valve against extremes of right or left.

The Role of the Military in Society and Government: Egypt* GEORGE KIRK

P. J. VATIKIOTIS, in the historical introduction to his recent work *The Egyptian Army in Politics*,[1] has made it clear that the relation of the military to society and government in Egypt is peculiar in that for many centuries, long before the Ottoman conquest in 1517, the inhabitants of the Nile Valley were largely exempt from military service. For instance, the Fatimids, the first important Muslim dynasty to be based upon Egypt (tenth to twelfth centuries, A.D.), depended for their military power "mainly on the services of Turks, Berbers, Nubians, and Armenians. Native Egyptians were never allowed to develop a tradition of military service or officer training, since neither was open to them."[2]

The exclusion of native Egyptians from employment as army officers continued during the five hundred years of Mamluk and Ottoman domination and through the eighteenth century; even when Muhammad Ali Pasha conscripted the Egyptian peasantry in his bid for independence of the Ottoman Empire in the 1830's, he continued to rely on non-Egyptians for his officer personnel. It was not until the short reign of

*The author wishes to acknowledge his indebtedness to P. J. Vatikiotis' work on this general subject and to indicate his extensive citing of passages from the particular volume mentioned. He does, however, assume sole responsibility for the choice of quotations and the conclusions drawn from them.

his son, Muhammad Sa'id (1854-63), that some officers' commissions were conferred on the sons of Egyptian village sheikhs; but this policy was so far reversed under Sa'id's successor, Isma'il, that as late as 1880, a numerically small group of native Egyptian colonels and majors found their further advancement blocked by the Turks and Circassians who monopolized the War Ministry and the higher ranks of the army. It was frustrated personal ambition, quite as much as ideals of reform, that led these native Egyptian officers to assume a leading political role in that incoherent and ill-directed movement of 1881-82 that took its name from Colonel Ahmad al-'Urābi.

Interpretation of the character of the 'Urābi movement have depended a good deal on the subjective standpoint of the writer essaying the interpretation. The more superficial of the British who brought about 'Urābi's downfall in 1882 saw the movement merely as a military revolt against lawful government and minimized its constitutional and reformist aspects. On the other hand, defenders of 'Urābi, like the romantic poet Wilfred Blunt, overemphasized the reformist element in 'Urābi and his colleagues and minimized the frenzied desire to protect themselves that led them into lawlessness and violence.[3] In our own time, Tom Little, a liberal British journalist strongly sympathetic to Gamal Abd al-Nasir, has seen 'Urābi as a rougher and less fortunate forerunner of his contemporary hero. So also has the French radical Jean Lacouture, but in a more discriminating and scholarly manner:

What the poor Egyptian army achieved between 1879 and 1882 was neither a putsch nor a pronunciamento, nor the brutal intervention of a military caste into the . . . life of the country. By rising against a privileged class of foreign origin and against Franco-British financial colonization, the "fellahin-officers" were expressing in an awkward, clumsy, and finally catastrophic fashion, the collective fevers of the nation of which they were the self-appointed representatives [les délégués spontanés], and whose feelings of humiliation and resentment they expressed with a special intensity.
. . . 'Urābi's attempt failed because he and his colleagues were hardly more than hot-blooded agitators, probably sincere but without political character or experience. . . .
. . . It was not then an upsurge of militarism but rather a popular uprising expressed, conducted, and finally misdirected by officers of plebeian origin.
. . . The populism of 'Urābi appears as a distant and crude preliminary sketch of Nasserism.[4]

For the next fifty years, the Egyptian army remained under British control or supervision. It was used mainly for frontier control against brigands and smugglers and was kept small. Some young men of wealthy Egyptian families who appreciated horsemanship, polo-playing, and similar sports were attracted by officers' commissions in the cavalry regiments; but careers in an army under the control of the occupying power had little patriotic prestige or attraction for the young urban middle-class Egyptians, who, during these fifty years, were graduating in increasing numbers from the high schools and the newer universities.[5] However, when the Anglo-Egyptian Treaty of 1936 advanced Egypt to sovereignty, the Egyptian government promptly enlarged the size of the army as a symbol of that sovereignty, and consequently increased the number of admissions of officer-cadets to the Military Academy.

It was to the classes of the years immediately after 1936 that Gamal Abd al-Nasir and his associates in the military coup of 1952 belonged;[6] and it is important to realize that some of them entered the Military Academy, not out of enthusiasm for a military career as such, but because that was the line of least resistance for them. In the period between the two world wars, the output of the Egyptian universities had been choking the labor market with graduates[7] for whom there were all too few openings in government service or the liberal professions, while commerce was largely monopolized by Europeans or members of the Christian and Jewish minorities. The young Muslim who lacked wealth, family influence, or academic distinction seemed doomed to stagnate in the growing white-collar proletariat of Cairo. It is evident from Gamal Abd al-Nasir's biographies that his high-school record was both academically weak and checkered by police convictions for political turbulence;[8] his father, a modest postmaster, had no resources for overcoming his son's indifferent start in life; and for the young Gamal Abd al-Nasir, as for the young Winston Churchill forty years earlier, the army seemed something of a last chance.

Once commissioned, these young Egyptian officers had the modest security of their lieutenant's pay but little constructive occupation. It is, indeed, never easy to find adequate occupation for infantry forces in peacetime, and Egypt remained non-belligerent throughout World War II; its army (except for the anti-aircraft units) was "an incidental accessory to the struggle of two alien forces,"[9] the British and the Axis.

73

Outdoor sports, which help to keep officers and men busy in the armies of countries with more temperate climates, had little appeal in torrid Egypt. Consequently, these young officers passed their all too abundant leisure in the same way as their civilian counterparts: in endless political gossip and scheming over their coffee cups. The tighter control exercised by Britain upon Egypt amid the emergencies of World War II naturally fanned their nationalist hatred of the occupying power; and, in addition, the underprivileged younger generation was increasingly disillusioned with the Egyptian party politicians who had selfishly exploited the constitutional regime set up in 1923:

> The whole urban lower middle class felt frustrated in its hopes and oppressed by a situation which placed public affairs in the hands of the few. Their bitterness was increased by the recollection of the struggle they had carried on in their student years in defense of political and social ideas in which they had sincerely believed, and which they now saw betrayed by the politicians who had exploited their youthful enthusiasms.[10]

As the military regime in Egypt has consolidated itself since 1952, its chroniclers and propagandists have tended to claim for its leaders a purposefulness at a very early stage of their careers. Thus, an official spokesman, in 1960, told the annual inflow of Fulbright Program personnel from the United States that "the Revolution was not the child of the moment. It took years to develop into what it was when it began, years of planning and providing for all eventualities."[11] But this is surely an extravagant claim. Vatikiotis is unquestionably correct when he states that

> between 1941 and 1949 there was no organized group of Free Officers. . . . The message was vague at this stage, for many of these officers continued to adhere or even belong to one or another of the organized political groups. . . .
> Any cohesion among these officers was based until 1949 entirely on their personal relations and contacts. . . . But it would be hasty to presume any ideological cohesion between these men in their early contacts, or any collective conspiracy based on neatly organized plans for revolutionary action.[12]

The year 1949 was a turning point: the humiliating defeats of the Egyptian army by the Israelis in the later stages of the Palestine war were a psychological shock which the officers tried to project upon others instead of analyzing the causes for themselves. Their propaganda declared that the Egyptian combat forces were "stabbed in the back" by

74

inefficient and corrupt supply services, the responsibility for which lay with the Cairo headquarters staff and with the Palace, and, further, that they were "deserted" by their Arab allies, notably by the Jordanians on the "treacherous" orders of King Abdullah and Glubb Pasha. But whatever degree of truth may attach to these charges, Abd al-Nasir's biographers make it clear that for him and his colleagues it was Britain, not the Israelis, who was Egypt's "Enemy No. 1" in 1948 and that, therefore, they went half-heartedly to war in Palestine. The memoirs of both Abd al-Nasir and former President Nagib bear artless testimony to the lack of organization and of *esprit de corps*, not only at headquarters, but in the Egyptian combat forces.[13] It had been, after all, sixty-six years since Egyptian troops had last been led into battle by Egyptian commanders. Inexperience, the lack of a military tradition, and a congenital unwillingness to accept responsibility made these officers no match for Israelis toughened by years of guerrilla fighting against both the Germans and the British (1944-47).

However, although the disastrous experience of the Palestine war caused Abd al-Nasir and his fellow malcontents among the junior officers to redouble their efforts to organize cells spreading subversive ideas within the army, there is no indication that they felt strong enough at this stage to make a bid for power on their own. It has been told that, in 1950, they had agreed on a five-year plan that fixed the date for revolution at 1954 or 1955[14]—a comfortably long time ahead; and when in the fall of 1951, the Wafdist Cabinet, to distract attention from its domestic misgovernment, plunged Egypt recklessly into guerrilla warfare against the British garrison in the Suez Canal Zone, Abd al-Nasir and his colleagues went along with the Wafd and gave practical support to the action.[15] The disastrous week in January, 1952, which saw the "battle" of Isma'iliya, Cairo's "Black Saturday," and the dismissal of the Wafdist government, was one more stage in the course of events that taught Abd al-Nasir and his colleagues that, if they were to act at all, they must act on their own; but their ideas were still far from clarified:

One looks in vain for a clear view of the role these officers envisaged for themselves even as late as 1951, other than resisting the King's abuses of their profession. One also finds few indications of any political program or plan of action. The fact that the Free Officers decided on a serious play for

power as late as March and July 1952 suggests that their chances for political success emerged only after civilian authority had collapsed. . . .
There were perhaps as many shades of political belief as there were members of the Free Officers Executive. Views ranged from extreme rightist, Islamic fundamentalist, and Fascist to left-wing radical socialist and Communist. Any contention therefore that the Society embraced a group of officers with a common ideological or political persuasion is erroneous.[16]

Abd al-Nasir claimed, in his *Philosophy of the Revolution,* originally published in 1954, that at the time of their expulsion of Faruq in July, 1952, he and his colleagues had regarded the role of the army as that of a "commando vanguard" that would have completed its task in a few hours, since the whole nation, ready and prepared, would fall in behind in "serried ranks, ready for the sacred advance towards the great objective." In reality, however, "the masses that came were disunited, divided groups of stragglers. The sacred advance toward the great objective was stalled."[17] Accordingly, the Free Officers' Executive that had planned the coup was soon reconstituted as the Revolutionary Command Council, and its members were appointed to executive positions controlling the departments of government. Once the Wafd and the other political parties had defied the Council's order to purge themselves of undesirable elements, they were declared dissolved, the Constitution of 1923 was abrogated, and a Liberation Rally inaugurated, primarily as a device "to clear out elements subversive to the regime from existing organizations among workers and students."[18] In the absence of any representative institutions, the military junta was primarily concerned, during 1952-54, with breaking the political power of the landowners through the long overdue agrarian reforms and with achieving the "national aspirations," where previous governments had failed, by compelling Britain to end her control of the Sudan and the Suez Canal Zone.

By July, 1954, this end was in sight, thanks largely to steady pressure on the British government from the overly optimistic United States Department of State; but the conditions that the military junta conceded to Britain as a *quid pro quo* for her withdrawal laid the regime open to attack from supporters of the Wafd, the widespread Muslim Brotherhood, the Communists, and other leftwingers. The attempt on Abd al-Nasir's life in October, 1954, expressed this domestic opposition, as the hanging of five leaders of the Muslim Brotherhood in December

76

symbolized the regime's determination to suppress it. The dropping of Nagib, the regime's "front man," from the presidency of the Republic, and his replacement by Abd al-Nasir, was one element in these internal struggles. "The popularity of General Naguib with his countrymen was not a practical source of strength sufficient to permit him to bypass the wishes of *the new power elite: the inner core of the Free Officers movement.*"[19] Furthermore, the emergence of this new power elite was already bringing about a shift in the social structure of Egypt. The army officers, as has been mentioned above, had been drawn, for the most part, from a more modest area of the middle class than that fraction which had enjoyed "upward mobility" along with the ascension of the political parties after World War I. The military coup of 1952 and the suppression of the parties was followed, temporarily, by a cult of austerity in public life; but it was observed that before long the ascendancy of the army officers was reflected in their own "upward mobility" in society, with some blurring of their former petty bourgeois simplicity.[20]

One important historical question that is not wholly clear is how far Abd al-Nasir's assumption of Pan-Arab leadership was a direct consequence of the removal from Egypt of the British incubus by the Anglo-Egyptian agreement of July–October, 1954,[21] or how far he was impelled to it by the need to regain credit as a patriot and nationalist after the Muslim Brotherhood's challenge to his authority. In either case, there is no doubt that the securing and retention of the leadership of the Pan-Arab movement was the prime occupation of the Egyptian military regime for the next three years. It was for this reason that the United Arab Republic was established, and for this reason that it meddled in the Lebanese crisis of 1958. This did not mean that the program of Egyptian domestic reform was abandoned during these years, but it was relegated to second place. The distribution of land to the peasantry under the agrarian reform continued, as did the organization of the rural co-operatives, the corollary of that reform.[22] Nevertheless, economic advantage was sometimes sacrificed to Abd al-Nasir's political *amour propre* and predilection for maneuver, notably his failure in 1956 to take up the joint United States and British offer, with the World Bank, to finance the first stage of the Aswan High Dam. Whatever may be said of Abd al-Nasir's arguments for delaying acceptance of the offer,[23] or of the reasons of the United States and British governments for eventually withdrawing it, there seems to be no doubt that Abd al-Nasir had reckoned too confidently on receiving a rival Soviet offer that would enable him to practice his so-called positive neutralism;[24] as a consequence, any beginning of work on the dam, ostensibly so vital to the economic development of Egypt,[25] was at a standstill for almost three years, between the announcement of the United States–British offer in December, 1955, and the announcement of the Soviet offer in October, 1958.

A similar verdict must be passed on the "Liberation Province" scheme, launched in December, 1953. Its director, a military officer, embarked on heavy capital expenditure and publicity promotion before making sure that there would be the necessary additional water resources from the high dam that was destined to be so long delayed. This was an error in planning comparable with that of the British Labour government's ill-fated East African ground-nuts scheme nearly ten years earlier; and that this error was not corrected until late in 1957, with the dismissal of the director and a drastic reduction of the Liberation Province's annual budget,[26] was due in all probability to the regime's distraction with its Pan-Arab policies and the ensuing Suez imbroglio in the previous two years.

In January, 1956, the Revolutionary Command Council promulgated a new constitution in fulfillment of its assurance, given in 1952, that the transition period following the abolition of the 1923 constitution should last only three years. The preamble and the first 192 articles of the 1956 constitution, drawn up by a panel of eminent Egyptian lawyers, were impeccably democratic in form; but the last section, entitled "Transitory and Final Rules" and consisting of only five articles, provided that the National Assembly (the body concerned with the exercise of legislative power and supposedly exercising control over the executive)[27] should be elected from candidates nominated by a Council of National Union, whose formation would be determined by the President of the Republic.[28] Since no candidate for the presidency other than Gamal Abd al-Nasir presented himself to the plebiscite of June, 1956, the authoritarian character of the regime was maintained behind this façade of democracy; and of the persons who later announced their candidacy for the National Assembly, no fewer than 46 per cent were disqualified by an executive committee consisting of three ministers who were members of the original military junta. The Assembly, elected after this preliminary screening, held forty-six meetings between July, 1957, and February, 1958, when it passed out of existence as a consequence of the merging of Egypt with Syria in the United Arab Republic. While its members had shown signs of independence of President Abd al-Nasir and his ministers,[29] the life of the Assembly was too short to indicate whether any significant trend away from authoritarian rule had been intended; and for the first two years of the United Arab Republic, any development of representative institutions was subordinated to the building-up of the National Union. It is to this concept, therefore, that attention should now be given.

To organize the National Union envisaged in the 1956 constitution, Abd al-Nasir chose one of his early collaborators, Colonel Anwar as-Sadat, who set out the purposes of the organization in a sixty-two-page booklet, *al-Ittihad al-Qawmi*. Amid a good deal of rhetoric, he provided glimpses of some of the probable preoccupations of the military regime in its relations with the people as a whole:

> The Revolution was first a secret organization, then a directing committee, then a government directing the people without recourse to an intermediary. Today our regime must be the government of the people by the people, freedom for the people to govern themselves and legislate for themselves, to propose and dispose, to judge others and themselves. . . .[30]
>
> Our Revolution took place without calling on the people to shed their blood or, if you like, without the people really sharing in the revolutionary experience. If then the people does not undergo change, then the Revolution will have achieved no purpose, great or small. What is important is not merely that the Revolution should suppress outworn regimes and replace them by strong young regimes, but that this action should be accompanied by an internal character-transformation, that values as well as regimes should undergo a fundamental renewal. . . .[31]
>
> We have truly succeeded in driving out colonialism, in winning our freedom and breaking the grip of the former corrupt governments. . . . but have we truly succeeded in destroying all the vitiated elements inside ourselves? . . . There are some among us who are still living as they did in the dead past, who are still harping on the same old tune. . . . and who consider personal sacrifice as a tax imposed upon them by the government. . . .[32]
>
> We must strengthen our position, our independence, our freedom, our neutralism, our Arabism. We shall not achieve this merely by getting all the people to rally behind the personality of President Gamal Abdul Nasir; we must also fuse them into a single organization which will direct our whole

people towards definite objectives. Without that, the Revolution will never be finally established. For as long as the President is merely the repository of the people's confidence—with an immense gap, devoid of any initiative that comes from the people and enjoys the confidence of the people, separating him from the various groups—so long will our interests, our independence, our freedom, our Arabism, and our neutralism remain in danger.[33]

The National Union was confirmed by Article 72 of the Provisional Constitution of the United Arab Republic, and elections to it were ordered for both the Egyptian and Syrian provinces in July, 1959. The decree provided for the formation of local councils, composed of representatives of villages, towns, and the quarters of cities, which would have certain powers in respect of taxation, education, health, and social affairs and a share in administration at the provincial level. Nevertheless, wrote a talented observer on the eve of this election,

> In spite of the effort of the rulers of the Republic to represent the National Union not as a party but as a popular movement comprising all tendencies and social classes and meeting the aspirations of everyone, it is difficult not to regard it as *a political organization functioning in the service of the official regime*. . . .
> By presenting itself in the guise of an organization that meets all the aspirations of the peoples of Syria and Egypt, the regime hopes to obtain a sort of unanimous vote of confidence to sanction it in the eyes of the Arab world, not only for the United Arab Republic but *for* the entire Arab world. And this regime is wholly embodied in the person of its unchallenged leader, Gamal Abd al-Nasir. . . .
> The National Union is in fact the creation of the Leader of the Egyptian revolution. He has complete control over it. It is he who lays down its program, names its secretary-general, its executive committee, its higher council, and places officials of the regime in charge of these organs, the heads of the governorates *(muhafaza)* being his own direct appointment. The election cannot fail to bear the stamp of the Head of the State. For if, at the lowest level of the "popular base," the National Union is to represent the free choice of the electors, the election of members of the higher councils and particularly of the Parliament will depend entirely and solely on President Abd al-Nasir.[34]

In fact, a retrospective study of the election revealed, as one of its probable purposes, the curtailing of the influence of the Ba'th party in Syria, whose opponents were allowed by the administration considerable freedom to campaign. In Egypt, on the other hand, the election was said to have been marked by "apathy and resignation" on the part of the voters.[35]

A general congress of 2,100 delegates of the National Union was held in Cairo in July, 1960. After three days spent in hearing speeches and reports from the President of the U.A.R. and his ministers for planning, foreign affairs, and defense, the delegates were divided into twenty-one committees to discuss, review, and make decisions on these reports. After four days of discussion, the twenty-one committees put forward 501 resolutions that were unanimously adopted by show of hands in a plenary meeting of the Congress; whereupon, the final session was held under the chairmanship of the President of the Republic, who five days later inaugurated a hand-picked 600-member National Assembly of the U.A.R.[36]

These exercises had their value in symbolizing the national unity to which the regime aspired, and they fulfilled an educational purpose for those taking part; but it was less easy to see in them more than an embryo of eventual consultative or deliberative organs of government. A not unsympathetic British researcher has written:

> When I was in the U.A.R. in 1960 I had the impression that no one took the National Union very seriously; certainly hardly anyone could give a clear description of its complex structure of committees and councils, although they were set out with detailed diagrams in many official leaflets and endlessly written up in the press, with the aim of popularizing the new system.[37]

For Vatikiotis, after manful attempts to elucidate the structure and organization of the National Union from its continuous revisions, one clear statement was

> that the National Union committees will have the right to accept or reject candidates to membership in various occupations and professional guilds, trade unions, local offices, and so forth. This in effect meant that no person not approved by the National Union would be able to participate in the governing or steering bodies of any groups in U.A.R. society.[38]

"It cannot be too frequently stressed," writes Vatikiotis, "that the Nasser regime did not depend for its essential power or position in the 1950's on positive popular support"; but he goes on to remark that "promises of new standards in political and economic performance"[39] have become an important device in the regime's efforts to secure popular acceptance. In another context, Vatikiotis emphasizes the importance that the regime evidently attaches to major policy speeches made at the annual congress of the Co-operative Unions;[40] and it was here, in December, 1957, that Abd al-Nasir enunciated the objective of establishing a "socialist, democratic, and cooperative society free from political, social, and economic exploitation." The chief defect to be eliminated from such a society was "opportunistic individualism";[41] but a year later Abd al-Nasir coupled "reaction" and "communism" together as enemies of his new ideal, and declared that the social system of the U.A.R. differed from that of the communist countries and that "in building a cooperative, democratic, socialist society we proclaim that we shall follow a policy of non-alignment, a policy that will deviate neither to the right nor the left."[42] In February, 1960, Abd al-Nasir emphasized that government in Egypt before the revolution had been dominated by private capitalism which had necessarily to be eliminated; and he referred to the National Planning Commission (established in 1957) as sharing in the capital of large concerns and controlling the principal sources of energy.[43]

During the Suez crisis of 1956, the Egyptian government decreed the nationalization of industrial and commercial concerns that were owned by citizens of the "aggressor" powers. By 1960, this government control had been extended to important sectors of the economy previously owned by citizens of the U.A.R., especially by members of the Greek, Lebanese, and Coptic Christian minorities. A writer in a government-controlled popular magazine explained that this policy differed from Soviet collectivization in that the government's desire to hasten economic development was coupled with the desire not to sacrifice private interests unduly:

> Today we come up against a sharp contradiction when we ask consumers to be both consumers and producers, to consume as little as possible and to produce the maximum. The Communists tell us that to resolve this contradiction we should establish an authoritarian regime and accustom the people to shortages and sacrifices for the sake of future generations. . . . We reject this view which is not in agreement with the character of our nation . . . .
> We cannot forget that the Arab nation has had an ancient civilization deeply rooted in the spirit of the people. The ordinary man, even though he is poor and uneducated, is still aware of the pride and glory of belonging to an ancient people. That is why he refuses to sacrifice his personality completely or to merge himself wholly in the mass.
> Hence it is wise to seek constantly to reconcile the pressing need of hasten-

82

ing development for the sake of society with the no-less pressing need of preserving human personality, in spite of the contradiction that this effort involves. . . .

To convince the individual that his interest and that of the nation must go together, that is the outcome of our democratic, socialist, and cooperative society. . . .[44]

The emphasis that the regime has placed in recent years on economic development, and especially on industrialization, has caused it to give greater responsibilities than formerly to professional economists, engineers, etc., drawn from the civilian population. Nevertheless, wrote Vatikiotis in 1960,

> Despite the elaborate cabinet system . . . , the intricate array of committees and commissions, ultimate responsibility and power still rest . . . with President Nasser and the small coterie of original Free Officers closest to him . . . Any civilian members of the Cabinet, however able and anxious to increase their share in power, have not been able to find easy access to civilian support. The National Union scheme of 1958-60 was strictly the creation and adjunct of the original army movement. Cabinet members have therefore been dependent for their continued participation in government on the sufferance of their Free Officer mentors.[45]

In this situation, the majority of intellectuals and professionals

> have claimed that they are willing to accept a transition period during which the government must "think for the people" until the people learn how to do so responsibly on their own. This . . . will come to pass after the public matures politically in the practical schools of the National Union scheme, national cooperatives, local councils, and the military service. Professionals and intellectuals in Egyptian society have further insisted that they are willing to defer to military leadership in this task because it has been able to provide, for the first time in the country's modern history, the psychological motivation of independence, dignity, and opportunity for constructive action . . .[46]

> Together with the Army Officer Corps, the President of the U.A.R. has gradually permitted a narrow section of society—some members of the group of professionals and intellectuals, the bureaucracy, and religious leaders—to share in government. . . . With the backing of some privileged members of these groups, President Nasser has been able to rule the passive masses, whose relative inertia made it easy to coerce them. . . . As a leading Egyptian historian put it to the author recently, "It is immaterial whether the Corps of Army Officers constitutes a distinct ruling elite or not. The masses must somehow adjust. They never understand the significance of even incipient representative institutions."

> Those of us who have recently visited and observed some of the Arab countries may argue that military regimes have infused into these societies

a new sense of order and national pride, made more purposeful by extensive plans for economic development and internal reform. At the same time, close study of the structure and organization of these governments fails as yet to provide satisfactory answers to such questions as public reponsibility and power, or to indicate more permanent characteristics of a stable political system. The ruler or "chief" continues to exercise almost unlimited authority . . . .[47]

Nadav Safran, who was born and had his early education in Egypt, has recently written that

the young authors of the revolution who have presided over Egypt's destinies for the last eight years came to power with no guiding political philosophy beyond a few generalities, and little in the way of a positive program beyond good intentions. They proceeded to work out philosophy and program in a pragmatic, experimental fashion, fighting at the same time against forces of reaction and counter-revolution and struggling among themselves for predominance in their own councils. The result was many false starts, mistaken courses, abrupt reversals, and a high degree of uncertainty.[48]

Abd al-Nasir's outstanding qualities, adds the Anglo-Lebanese George Hourani,

are his great zeal and strong will . . . combined with a sincere dedication to the well-being of his country. . . .

Nasir's limitations reflect the shortcomings of his education and experience. His power of expression is not above average. He lacks the finesse of the upper-class Egyptian.[49]

In these respects, a middle-aged European conservative like the present writer sees a likeness to Benito Mussolini, who nearly forty years ago similarly

promised law and order, a full appreciation of victory and its worth, an Italy cured of poverty, restored to its dignity, resuming its place among the great nations of Europe, and governed by youth and youthful energy.[50]

The Duce's later embarkation upon the imperial projects that led him to his ruin was largely due to the intractability of his domestic problem; and in somewhat similar fashion the writing on the wall appeared, during 1961, for the Egyptian *Ra'is*. A British special correspondent, who visited Egypt that summer, commented on "the feeling of self-confidence—self-importance, perhaps—that is one of the most marked qualities of contemporary Egypt," despite the vagueness of the "magic formula" of Arab socialism that had just been supplemented by another wide range of nationalization measures embracing virtually every aspect of the United Arab Republic's economy.[51] The correspondent concluded:

> No doubt the regime's shortcomings are plain. There is still corruption. Thought is controlled and dissent stifled. It is a philistine regime. It arose out of an Army conspiracy, and at the top it is still secretive and exclusive. A clash of wills inside the junta is one thing which could conceivably upset President Nasser. The other is the defection of Syria. Neither seems at all likely. . . .[52]

Six weeks later, however, the Syrian army officers and propertied class had combined to reject Egyptianization and economic control, and had compelled Abd al-Nasir to accept the defection of his "northern province." The Pan-Arab unity of which he had recently spoken as "something that is bound to happen"[53] lay in ruins about him. To offset the blow to his prestige, he told the Egyptian public in a broadcast address on October 16 that the regime

> had made the mistake . . . of failing to identify reaction correctly: "We were striking our blows at imperialism in the shape of pacts and bases, while imperialism had already changed its place and had hidden in palaces and in the safes of millionaires." Secondly, . . . the National Union . . . had been infiltrated by reaction. Third, there had not been enough popular consciousness of what the revolution meant. Fourth, they had carried on with the old Government machinery. . . .[54] The social revolution requires increased revolutionary socialism.[55]

The property of 850 "capitalist reactionaries who had . . . exploited their funds for their own selfish interest or smuggled them out of the country"[56] was sequestrated, and immediate measures were announced to improve conditions for the poor and lower-middle classes. At the same time, Abd al-Nasir announced an involved procedure for electing a council of "representatives of real and genuine forces of the people" to consider a "charter for national action" prepared by the President, on the basis of which a general conference of the National Union—thus overhauled for the fourth time—would be elected in two stages and charged with producing a permanent constitution for the "United Arab Republic."[57]

The conclusion is that after nine years the Egyptian military regime has not yet succeeded in associating the non-political mass of the population with itself in any positive manner. This must be discouraging to those over-ardent prophets who not long ago saw in Abd al-Nasir and his regime the "wave of the future" for the Arab world;[58] but it is no surprise to those historians who are aware of the millennial passivity, interspersed with suspicion, which the Egyptian masses have shown to their rulers.[59] During these past nine years, the regime has doubtlessly learned by hard experience to appreciate better the extent of the politico-economic and psychological problems facing it. Behind closed doors, Abd al-Nasir and his colleagues may indulge in salutary self-criticism. Nevertheless, their task is not made easier by their recurrent tendency to seek public scapegoats for their own errors and to conceal the inevitable shortcomings of the present behind a cloud of extravagant promises for the future.[60] But this is an age of demagogy everywhere; Egypt is, according to her present rulers, a part of Africa; and it was presumably Africa that furnished the material for that Ivory Gate to the underworld that Vergil described:

> polished, of ivory white, but *false* the dreams
> there wafted upwards from the world of shades.[61]

1. Bloomington, Ind.: Indiana University Press, 1961.
2. *Ibid.*, p. 4.
3. Cf. the Congolese *soldateska* of 1960-61.
4. "Le nasserisme et l'uniforme," *Etudes Méditerranéennes*, No. 8 (November, 1960). See also a version of the article in *New Outlook*, IV, No. 5 (March–April, 1961), 4-5.
5. "Ten years ago when a middle- or upper-class youth viewed military service as strictly the job of the illiterate and impoverished *fellah*, or peasant.."—Vatikiotis, *op. cit.*, p. 232.
6. For details see *ibid.*, pp. 48-49, 54-55.
7. Nadav Safran, *Egypt in Search of Political Community* (1961), p. 207.
8. Robert St. John, *The Boss: The Story of Gamal Abdul Nasser* (1960), chap. iii.
9. Mahmoud Manzalawi, *Middle East Forum*, XXXVII, No. 8 (October, 1961), 17.
10. Paolo Minganti, *L'Egitto Moderno* (Florence, 1959), pp. 159-60. See also Safran, *op. cit.*, p. 195, who writes, "a social policy which, for its one-sidedness and selfishness, had very few rivals in modern times."
11. Amin Shaker, "Interview with the Fulbright Professors," *Arab Review*, I, No. 7 (1960), 57.
12. Vatikiotis, *op. cit.*, pp. 56-57.
13. St. John, *op. cit.*, chap. v; Mohammed Nagib, *Egypt's Destiny* (1955), pp. 22-27.

14. St. John, *op. cit.*, p. 110; Jean and Simonne Lacouture, *Egypt in Transition* (1958), p. 143; Vatikiotis, *op. cit.*, pp. 60 ff.

15. Anwar Sadat, *Revolt on the Nile* (1957), pp. 101-4; Lacouture, *op. cit.*, pp. 142-43; St. John, *op. cit.*, p. 99. Vatikiotis' denial (*op. cit.*, p. 65) may be derived from a later piece of "new-speak" on the part of the Egyptian propaganda machine.

16. Vatikiotis, *op. cit.*, pp. 67-68. Their choice of a senior officer, General Muhammad Nagib, as their public "front" is one indication of the diffidence felt by these thirty-year-olds in a society that has traditionally associated wisdom with seniority and experience.

17. *Philosophy of the Revolution* (English translation, 1955), pp. 32-33. For a claim that the officers had originally intended to return to their barracks six months after the coup, see Vatikiotis, *op. cit.*, p. 85.

18. Vatikiotis, *op. cit.*, p. 283 n. 1.

19. *Ibid.*, p. 90 (emphasis added).

20. Lacouture, *op. cit.*, pp. 287-88 (the original French edition was published in 1956) : Keith Wheelock, *Nasser's New Egypt* (1960), pp. 47-48; Vatikiotis *op. cit.*, p. 123.

21. Some prefaces contributed by Abd al-Nasir to official publications in 1954 (see Jean Vigneau in W. Z. Laqueur, *Middle East in Transition* [1958], pp. 137-38) point to this conclusion; but since Abd al-Nasir was employing ghost writers, some of these views may have originally been theirs rather than their over-worked leader's.

22. A. M. Goichon, "Le plan de rénovation sociale de la campagne égyptienne," *Orient* (Paris), Nos. 17-20 (1961).

23. See his speech of July 26, 1956, announcing the nationalization of the Suez Canal, Royal Institute of International Affairs, *Documents on International Affairs*, 1956, pp. 97-102.

24. James B. Dougherty, "The Aswan Decision in Perspective," *Political Science Quarterly*, LXXIV (1959), 22-24.

25. But compare Sir Hamilton Gibb, "Egyptians are well aware that it will not solve Egypt's economic problems; but it is a symbol of the new determination of Egyptians to control for themselves the economic organization and destinies of their country, and, therefore, it already effectively exists before a single stone has been put in place" (in Tibor Kerekes [ed.], *The Arab Middle East and Muslim Africa* [1961], p. 17).

26. Arnold Hottinger, "Egypt's 'Liberation Province'—Another Planning Failure," *Swiss Review of World Affairs*, VIII, No. 9 (December, 1958).

27. Articles 65 and 66.

28. Article 192.

29. J. Harris Proctor, "The Legislative Activity of the Egyptian National Assembly of 1957-8," *Parliamentary Affairs* (London), Vol. XIII, No. 2 (1960) ; Simon Jargy, "La Syrie à la veille d'une nouvelle expérience," *Orient* (Paris), No. 10 (1959).

30. Excerpts translated by André Miquel, "L'union nationale," *Orient* (Paris), No. 8 (1958), p. 160.

31. *Ibid.*, p. 164.

32. *Ibid.*, pp. 164-65.

33. *Ibid.*, pp. 161-62.

34. Jargy, *op. cit.*, pp. 28-29 (emphasis in the original).

35. Simon Jargy, "Le déclin d'un parti," *Orient* (Paris), No. 11, (1959), p. 32.

36. *The Arab Review*, Vol. I, No. 6 (August, 1960); George Vaucher, *Gamal Abdel Nasser et son équipe, (L'édification de la République Arabe Unie*, Vol. II [1960]), p. 324.

37. J. S. F. Parker, "The United Arab Republic," *International Affairs*, No. 38 (1962), pp. 22-23.

38. Vatikiotis, *op. cit.*, p. 113, and cf. p. 107; Vaucher, *op. cit.*, pp. 333-34.

39. Vatikiotis, *op. cit.*, p. 102.

40. *Ibid.* pp. 139, 286 n. 23.

41. Wheelock, *op. cit.*, p. 69.

42. Speeches of November and December, 1958; see *Oriento Moderno*, No. 38 (1958), p. 981, and *Orient* (Paris), No. 8 (1958), pp. 188-89, translated from *al-Ahram* of November 15 and December 24, 1958, respectively. For the increasing use of colloquial Egyptian Arabic in the reporting of Abd al-Nasir's speeches see Paolo Minganti, "Note sull'uso del dialetto nella stampa quotidiana in Egitto," *Oriente Moderno*, No. 41 (1961), pp. 502-6.

43. *Orient* (Paris), No. 13 (1960), pp. 157-61, translated from *al-Ahram*, February 3, 1960.

44. Fathi Ghanim, "Our Socialism Compared with Capitalism and Communism," *Rosa'l-Yusuf*, February 13, 1961; French translation in *Orient* (Paris), No. 18 (1961), pp. 179-80. "Between the avarice of the extreme right and the deviations of the extreme left the interests of the people are lost."—Jamal Mohammad Ahmed, *The Intellectual Origins of Egyptian Nationalism* (1960), p. 126, quoting from *al-Ahram*, June 30, 1959.

45. Vatikiotis, *op. cit.*, p. 222; and Vaucher, *op. cit.*, p. 333.

46. Vatikiotis, *op. cit.*, p. 220; and Mohammad Diab, "The Economic System of the UAR: Where Is It Going?", *Middle East Forum*, XXXVII, No. 6 (June, 1951), 19-20.

47. Vatikiotis, *op. cit.*, pp. 255-57.

48. Safran, *op. cit.*, p. 253.

49. In Kerekes, *op. cit.*, p. 40.

50. Laura Fermi, *Mussolini* (1961), p. 215; Vatikiotis, *op. cit.*, p. 257.

51. Hans-Jürgen Kornrumpf, "Die neue Ordung in der VAR," *Orient* (Hamburg), II, No. 5 (October, 1961), 205: "It is impossible to avoid the impression that many of the new decrees were faultily prepared and hastily promulgated."

52. "Egypt Grows Mellow with Success," *Times* (London), August 24, 1961.

53. *Ibid.*

54. Already in August, Abd al-Nasir's advisers had been speaking of the failure of "the old cadres," "the old elites," and "the old intelligentsia" (Dana Adams Schmidt, *New York Times*, August 13, 1961).

55. "Old Bogy in New Clothes," editorial in the *Times* (London), October 24, 1961.

56. Dispatch from Cairo, *Ibid.*, October 23, 1961.

57. "Pres. Nasser's Sop to the Egyptians," *ibid.*, November 6, 1961; Jay Walz, "Nasser Is Pushing 'Popular Powers,'" *New York Times*, December 10, 1961.

58. See, for example, Harry B. Ellis, *Challenge in the Middle East* (1960) pp. 211-12, 221-22.

59. H. A. R. Gibb and Harold Bowen, *Islamic Society and the West*, I, Part I (1950), 215, 264.

60. Notably, the objective of doubling the standard of living in ten years, which Abd al-Nasir proclaimed in the summer of 1959. See Wheelock, *op. cit.*, pp. 151-52.

61. *Aeneid* vi. 895-96 (translation of Charles J. Billson [1924]).

The Role of the Military in Society and Government in Israel J. C. HUREWITZ

THE ROLE OF THE MILITARY in society and government in Israel is an especially timely subject, for throughout most of 1961 the country was wracked by a political crisis over military-government relations. The political crisis began with the resignation of Prime Minister David Ben Gurion on January 31, 1961, over the so-called Lavon Affair, a dispute that hinged on the management of the Defense Ministry by Pinhas Lavon, the only man other than Ben Gurion who has ever held that office. On November 2, the *Kneset* (legislature) finally gave its blessing to Ben Gurion's new cabinet, still dominated by his Mapai (Israel Labor party) ; but it took eleven weeks of stiff bargaining with the other parties of the outgoing government, two of which ultimately refused to come back, before the new coalition was nailed together. In the election campaign for the fifth Kneset, and particularly in the negotiations for the new government, the smaller parties charged Ben Gurion with abusing his powers over the armed forces. He was accused of resorting to authoritarian practices by failing to consult his ministerial colleagues or to inform the legislature in advance of basic policy decisions on military and security affairs. The survival of Israel's democracy, it was contended, could be assured only by institutionalizing

89

civilian mastery over the armed forces at the executive and legislative levels.

The smaller parties of the expiring coalition tried to wring from Mapai the right to share in the handling of security matters. They demanded the surrender by Mapai of its customary majority in multiple-party cabinets and the modification of its invariable rule of assigning to Mapai members the key ministries of Defense, Finance, and Foreign Affairs. They also insisted on the introduction of institutional controls, at the cabinet and Kneset levels, over the management of the Ministry of Defense and over policies affecting the armed forces and the country's security. They specifically proposed that in the future the Defense Ministry should be accountable, in the cabinet, to a security committee invested with full policy-making authority and, in the Kneset, to the existing Committee on Foreign Affairs and Security endowed with broad investigative powers, including the right to subpoena any officer in the armed forces or any official in the Defense Ministry without, as in the past, having first to seek the ministry's approval.

It is perhaps worth noting that some were specifically advocating the creation within the cabinet of a National Security Council roughly patterned after that in the United States. These critics gave no evidence of having pondered the essential differences between the parliamentary and presidential systems. For in the American government, the National Security Council could be nothing more than a presidential advisory body; but the Israel advocates were insisting that their projected variant should be given exclusive policy-making powers over defense affairs. Similarly, in place of the existing Kneset committee system, based on that in Britain where Parliamentary commitees deal mainly with legislation, the Israel proponents of reform were urging the adoption of the practice developed by the American Congress, whose committees enjoy the widest investigative powers.

The demand for such reforms received the endorsement of the newly created non-socialist Liberal party and the two non-communist Marxist parties—the Ahdut ha-'Avodah (Labor Unity party) and the pro-Soviet Mapam (United Labor party). Mapam added yet another demand: the immediate abolition of military administration in the Arab areas. In the end, only one of the three parties, Ahdut ha-'Avodah, agreed to enter the new government with the promise of the formation

90

of a Ministerial Security Committee comprising the ministers of Foreign Affairs, Finance, Agriculture (all three ministers belonging to Mapai), Labor (Ahdut ha-'Avodah), and Interior (National Religious party) under Ben Gurion's chairmanship. The Minister of Agriculture, Moshe Dayan, was manifestly selected because he had served as chief of the General Staff, and the Minister of Labor, Yigal Allon, because he had led the three commando brigades in Israel's war with the Arab states in 1948. The Ministerial Security Committee was established as an advisory body with the right to request information on and to discuss—on the initiative of the Defense Minister, the cabinet, or any member of the committee—the direction of all aspects of security affairs from military planning and operations to arms purchases and weapons development. Its power to investigate, however, was severely circumscribed: only those military officers and Defense Ministry officials authorized by the Defense Minister might appear before the Military Security Committee for interrogation.[1]

But the incipient cabinet committee, modeled after one that functioned until a few years ago, was expressly denied policy-making authority; the investigative powers of the Kneset Committee on Foreign Affairs and Security were not widened; and the Arab districts remained under military administration. Thus at the year's close, although a new government was erected—albeit on a smaller coalition base than the old and with less support in the Kneset—none of the fundamental military-government issues, as contested in the election and in the formation of the new cabinet, was resolved.

Those parties that charged that Israel's democracy was being trampled by the armed forces under the "authoritarian" leadership of the aging Ben Gurion were not likely to change their views or their tactics. Nor might Mapai be expected to cease extolling the vigor of Israel's democracy, confirmed—as it contended—by the fall of the cabinet over the very issue of civilian control of the military establishment and by the consequent free public discussion of the entire range of civil-military relations in the election campaign and after. Nevertheless, the final compromise, modest as it was, suggested that civilian checks on the armed forces were perhaps neither as inclusive nor as firmly fixed as many Israelis might have wished. It was no less clear that the smaller parties that had sat in earlier coalition governments were using the defense issue hopefully as a means of undermining the power of Mapai. Before an attempt is made to evaluate the way in which the military establishment has related itself to the government, it would be helpful to take a look at Israel's security position and the structure of its armed forces.

Israel's security problems are perhaps too well known for detailed rehearsal. But an appreciation of their magnitude is indispensable to an appraisal of the state's defense efforts. A frontier of 750 miles—four-fifths of it on land—is uncommonly long for a country less than 8,000 square miles in size; the central coastal plain, for a distance of some thirty-five miles, is scarcely wider than a dozen miles; no point within Israel is more than ten minutes by slow, propeller-driven plane from a hostile land frontier; and the Mediterranean coast apart, Israel has no permanent boundaries. By resorting to economic and political blockade practices, the Arab governments continue to seek to isolate Israel. The state was born in a war for survival, and its neighbors have not yet given up the aspirations of wiping Israel off the Middle East map. Of this objective the Israelis are reminded almost daily on the air and in the press by responsible Arab spokesmen.

"You are at the moment seated," Brigadier General Hayyim Herzog, Director of Military Intelligence, opened his address on military censorship in Israel before delegates to the International Press Institute conference at Tel-Aviv on May 30, 1961,

> within the range of the medium artillery of an army whose government [Jordan] maintains that it is in a state of war with Israel. Had your original plan been carried out, namely to meet in Herzliyah a few miles north of here, you would have been within field artillery range of the guns of the self-same army. When you visit the Knesset [in Jerusalem] you will be within light mortar range and in some Government offices you will be in pistol range.[2]

This may sound like overdramatization to some, but not to Israel's security planners, who are acutely conscious of their state's vulnerability and who argue that Israel cannot afford to lose a war, since it may never have a second chance. These menacing realities go far to explain the government's undiminished suspicion toward its Arab minority, which, located in part along the armistice lines, remains basically sympathetic to the state's enemies and thus forms a potentially subversive force. Yet some Israelis—among them, Mapam was the largest group—disagreed with their government's Arab policy, particularly with the treatment of the Arab minority, on ideological grounds and insisted that Israel would have to take the initiative in abandoning the residual military administration. But these views, though articulate, did not prevail, and the government's policy seemed still to command the public's mandate.

Continued mutual distrust gave rise, as one of the complicating results, to a steady and brisk arms race between the Arab states and Israel. If the rivals had been left to their own devices, Israel would still enjoy a technological lead over its neighbors. But early in life Israel developed a sense of isolation that reached its greatest intensity in the winter of 1955-56, when the Soviet bloc began competing with the Western countries in courtship of the Arab states by the grant or sale of modern military equipment. This importation of military hardware that Israel could neither make nor buy had the effect of a technological breakthrough by its Arab enemies. Isolation came to an end in the summer and fall of 1956 as a result of the Suez crisis, which aligned France and Britain against Egypt and brought Israel early delivery of jets long on order from France. Israel's pre-emptive strike in Sinai might by attributed largely to its fixed purpose of restoring a qualitative-weapons lead by the destruction or capture of much of Egypt's Soviet Bloc equipment, which was conveniently, if threateningly, stockpiled along Israel's southwest frontier.

Internal difficulties further jeopardized Israel's security. Israel, for the most part, was a land of immigrants who arrived after the declaration of independence. To the 650,000 Jews living there in May, 1948, were added by 1961 a million newcomers. Some two-thirds came in the first three and one-half years; the rest at a more leisurely pace in the next ten. Until the settlers were integrated into the society and economy, they represented more of a liability than an asset. They did not know the terrain; they spoke different languages; and their dedication to the country's mission of sponsoring the Jewish national renaissance and to the sacrifices that state-building entailed was untested. Asians and Africans in the majority, they hailed from countries of low living standards, and not a few were illiterate. Their assimilation was costly. There was no certainty that the standards of the Asians and

Africans would be lifted or those of the Europeans lowered. As in most countries in Asia and Africa, the developing economy was competing with the defense establishment for the same limited resources. Every pound that went into weapons—except for saleable exports of local manufacture—was a pound taken away from economic expansion. Moreover, the multiple-party system carried with it the possibility of deadlock and consequent paralysis of leadership.

In these circumstances, Israel faced the need to create a military establishment that would provide maximal use of its technical and managerial skills at a minimal cost in manpower and funds, so as not to hamper the expanding economy. Its armed forces would have to be capable of rapid mobilization and demobilization. It would have to achieve and preserve a qualitative superiority in weapons over the armies of its neighbors, and to do so with the least dependence on the outside—in view of the unreliability of external sources of supply— while cultivating as many foreign powers as possible in the outer, non-Arab zone of the Middle East and in Asia and Africa, no less than in Europe and America. The army would have to furnish a means of integrating the heterogeneous, polyglot immigrants into the society and populating the repellent districts on the frontier and in the desert. The founders of Israel's defense establishment sought to foster all these purposes; and, to a remarkable degree, they succeeded. What techniques did they employ?

Israel found its primary answer in a citizen army. The structure of the Defense Army of Israel *(Zva Haganah le-Israel* or Zahal) is more typical of Europe than the Middle East; and, among the European armies, Zahal—particularly in the organization of the reserves—most closely resembles the citizen army of Switzerland, after which it was originally patterned. Yet, in time, Zahal developed its own distinctive qualities, partly inherited from a pre-independence, semilegal militia, and partly adapted from British, French, American, and Russian practices to meet the special security needs of the country.

In 1948, a hodgepodge of military units that had come into being in the Jewish community under the mandate fought what has since been designated the War for Liberation. Haganah (defense), the largest group, was essentially a secret militia organized by the Jewish quasi-government in 1921, and progressively enlarged in later years, in

94

co-operation with and in defiance of the Palestine government; by 1948, it could place about 45,000 troops in the field. Two smaller, dissident, political terrorist groups—the National Military Organization *(Irgun Zvai Leumi)*, which numbered about 3,000, and the Fighters for Israel's Freedom *(Lohamei Herut Israel)*, which numbered less than 500, formed in 1938 and 1940, respectively—did not acknowledge the quasi-government's jurisdiction, although at various times after the summer of 1945 they co-operated with Haganah. In less than a fortnight after the declaration of independence, the Provisional Government of Israel issued a special ordinance establishing the Defense Army of Israel. Within the area assigned to the Jewish state by the UN General Assembly's partition resolution, the Irgun and the Freedom Fighters were declared illegal and their members compelled to join Zahal. The terrorist groups, however, continued their independent action in the Jerusalem area until they were finally disbanded in September, 1948, immediately after the murder of Count Bernadotte, the UN Palestine Mediator. The depoliticization of the armed forces was completed early in November with the dissolution of the headquarters of Palmah,[3] Haganah's commando troops, who were closely identified with the collective villages of Ahdut ha-'Avodah.

The Kneset enacted on September 8, 1949—less than two months after the consummation of the Arab-Israel armistice system—a comprehensive Defense Service Law,[4] which, with later amendments, established the legal basis of Israel's citizen army. The Defense Army of Israel embraces the ground troops, the navy, and the air force. The Regular Service *(Sherut Sadir)*, or the troops on active duty, consists of the professional forces and the conscripts in the three branches. The professional forces constitute what is called the Permanent Service *(Sherut Quevah)*. In the army, the Permanent Service is composed of no more than a nucleus of commissioned and noncommissioned officers who form the cadre for the reserve units and carry out functions of command, planning, administration, technical service, and instruction. Because of the need for constant preparedness, and for special servicing and maintenance, the Permanent Service of the navy and air force represents a much larger proportion of their total manpower.

The rank and file of the Regular Service is made up of the Conscript Service *(Sherut Hovah)* which, under the law, all men and women [5]

95

on reaching eighteen years of age must enter, the men for thirty months and the women for twenty-four.[6] Because of the large number of immigrants of military age still pouring into the country in those early years, liability for the draft continued until the age of twenty-nine, although the term for recruits above twenty-six was reduced to twenty-four months for men and eighteen for women. The army conscripts form infantry components that, when not in training or on maneuver, are normally assigned to border patrol. Upon completion of their terms of service, the draftees enter the Reserve Service *(Sherut Miluim)*, composed of all able-bodied men under forty-five and unmarried women under thirty-five. Based on designated military districts, the reserve formations are issued emergency equipment, including vehicles. Men under forty are liable for an uninterrupted month of training each year, and older men for two weeks, with each age group reporting for duty the equivalent of one day a month. All commissioned and noncommissioned officers must additionally serve one consecutive week each year. After June 1, 1953, all men between the ages of forty-five and forty-nine constituted the Civil Defense *(Hitgonenut Ezrahit)*.

Israel developed a military doctrine that called for the fusion of strategic, economic, and Zionist ideological purposes by erecting fortified villages inhabited by specially chosen and prepared personnel along the exposed frontier. Comparably recruited were volunteers for settling uncultivated farm land and other areas in the country that might be uninviting for reasons of climate or remoteness. Before independence, this function had been performed by the Zionist-socialist youth movements, whose members reached Palestine after protracted training— often of six or more years' duration—in their native lands. The Defense Service Law of 1949 simply allocated this task to the army.

In the early years, all recruits, except those electing to serve in the air force and the navy, were sent, after basic military training, for agricultural training to frontier villages for the rest of their terms. They also underwent instruction in socialism for living in co-operative and collective villages. These trainees were called the Fighting Pioneer Youth *(No'ar Haluzi Lohem* or Nahal). Because there was non-socialist resistance to the use of universal military service as an agency for propagating socialism, Nahal was transformed, in the mid-1950's, from an obligatory into a voluntary instrument. In the first year on the farm,

Nahal members had to devote five days a month to refresher military training, and in the second year the same time to advanced training. Nahal shored up the defense of the exposed frontier by assuring a steady, if rotational, supply of infantry, providing candidates for permanent residence in existing but understaffed border villages, and funneling recruits into new security villages. Every male farmer in an Israel frontier village is a disciplined soldier. Every village is equipped with appropriate defense weapons and essential stores of food, fuel, medical supplies, and underground shelters. Neighboring villages in the exposed districts are organized for mutual support; and, in an emergency, reinforcements are swiftly available from the nearest towns. Ghana and Burma's interest in the concept of Nahal suggests its wider applicability in newly independent states with border problems.

Volunteers for Nahal and for the air force and navy are sought among members of Gadna (*Gdudei No'ar* or youth battalions), a premilitary movement first established early in World War II and placed, in 1949, under the combined direction of Zahal and the ministries of Defense and of Education and Culture. Gadna attempts to reach all youngsters between fourteen and seventeen, whether in school or already employed. Through weekly unit meetings, periodic camp exercises, and an eleven-day basic-training program, the government endeavors to instil patriotism in the youth and to develop a sense of loyalty to the purposes of the citizen army.

Israel's navy has operated almost wholly in the Mediterranean. Although the Gulf of 'Aqabah was opened up in 1956, it has had no practical naval use since it lacks adequate maintenance and repair facilities and is inaccessible for joint maneuvers or action with Israel's Mediterranean vessels. Modest in size, the navy still comprises chiefly frigates, destroyers, and torpedo boats. In 1960, Israel acquired two submarines from Britain and trained the necessary personnel in the United Kingdom. The air force procured its first jets in 1955. By 1960, all fighting aircraft were jet-propelled, among them Vautours and Super-Mystères.

The army, the navy, and the air force are represented in a single general staff, headed by a chief of staff who may be an officer from any one of the three branches but who so far has always been drawn from the army. The general staff consists additionally of the chiefs of manpower, logistics, and intelligence; the commanders of the air force, navy, and armor; the officers commanding the northern, the central, and the southern area commands; and the director of military training. Of the half-dozen officers—three members of Mapai, two independents, and one General Zionist—who have risen to the rank of chief of staff, all except the first were younger than forty on appointment and—the present incumbent apart—were retired into civilian employment before reaching the age of forty-two. In their civilian jobs they are, moreover, distributed in the country's three command areas, so that in time of emergency they might put their command experience to the most effective use.

The Ministry of Defense owns and runs all factories producing military equipment. From these plants have come a mounting variety of weapons, spare parts, and communications equipment. The military industry has deliberately cultivated the export market, and, in 1960, sold some 30 per cent of the total production abroad, earning hard currency for the purchase of strategic raw materials and capital equipment for further expansion. The Ministry's Research and Planning Department, which boasts the largest laboratories in the country, while primarily concerned with weapons research, has also developed electronic devices for military and civilian use. A modest aircraft industry, Bedek, has been launched. Starting out as an agency servicing the air force and local and foreign airlines, Bedek also became a hard-currency earner and thus could take care of its own replacement and expansion needs. It has been manufacturing, under French license, jet-propelled training planes.

Druzes and Circassians have been the country's only non-Jews to join Zahal from the very outset. The Druzes of military age, at their own request, became subject to compulsory service in 1956; and the practice was later extended to the Circassians. Wholly exempt from the draft are the Arabs—Christian and Muslim. Indeed, Arabs are not even permitted to volunteer for Zahal. Nor would they do so in significant numbers, even if allowed, since they can hardly be expected to approve the state's central purpose of fostering Jewish nationalism.

As a domestic function, the Israel army remained ultimately responsible for administering the areas of concentrated Arab population. The Arab citizens in these districts—more than four-fifths of the 240,000 in the land—do not enjoy free mobility and must carry identification cards on their persons. The actual supervision of these regulations has been taken over progressively by the civilian police. Yet, still in effect are drastic emergency laws, originally promulgated by the mandatory government to hold in check political violence by Arabs and Jews. For crimes committed under these laws, Arabs are tried by military courts. The sentences require the commanding general's endorsement, from which there is no appeal. Under Kneset legislation, first adopted in 1954, unauthorized movement in either direction across the armistice lines is an offense that is judged by a one-man military court, from which an appeal may be made, not to a civilian court, but only to a three-man military one.[7]

But some cases of this sort do not even reach the military courts, for the army patrols the frontiers vigilantly. This was illustrated by the shooting, in September, 1961, of five young Arabs who attempted to cross into the Egyptian-administered Gaza Strip at night. The incident gave rise to the most vigorous anti-government Arab demonstrations since 1948. The government position was best explained by Minister of Agriculture Moshe Dayan, chief of staff at the time of the Sinai War, who pointed out that the military authorities suspected the young Arabs of planning to join *fidaiyun* or commando units for later sabotage and espionage against Israel. "The defense of our frontiers against infiltrators," observed Dayan, "is one of our toughest security problems. There are neither natural obstacles, such as rivers or mountains, nor artificial ones, such as mined barbed wire fences. . . ."[8]

In Israel's citizen army, there are easy working relations between the officers and the recruits, an eschewal of formalistic discipline, and a high degree of individual initiative even among the ranks. In these respects, Zahal closely parallels the Swiss army as so well described by Frederick Martin Stern, who writes that[9]

> the Swiss have entirely sacrificed that splendor so dear to the adherents of the good old traditional armies. . . . The troops always look and act with an informality which the officers of most armies would forgive only in the combat zone. . . . The Swiss do not take it easy, nor do they stint themselves on modern equipment, but their army is strictly a "utility" army.
>
> The Swiss system is not cheap, but it is extremely economical. . . .

The capabilities of Israel's defensive army in offensive operations were tested in Sinai in 1956. As General S. L. A. Marshall has so vividly described, Israel could, within seventy-two hours, mobilize for action five reserve brigades and three conscript brigades; and, as he pointed out, the men of one of the reserve brigades were back to their farms within eleven days of call-up.[10]

How does Israel's citizen army relate itself to the government? Israel has no written constitution. Neither the Law and Administration Ordinance of May 19, 1948, nor the Transition Law of February 16, 1949—which provides basic constitutional guidance on the allocation of powers among the executive, the legislature, and the judiciary—sheds any light on the question of civilian control over the armed forces. Still, the Defense Minister is responsible, under all legislation on the armed forces, for executing the laws and issuing all attendant regulations; and the Defense Minister has always been a civilian. Moreover, all proposed legislation, that pertaining to the defense establishment included, although drafted in the pertinent ministry or ministries, must receive cabinet approval before it is sent to the Kneset. There ample opportunity obtains, in the three plenary readings and in the intervening committee review, for rejection or modification. While the annual budget of the Defense Ministry, which administers all allocations to the armed forces, does not reach the floor of the Kneset for reasons of security, it must, nevertheless, receive the approval of the Kneset committees on Finance and on Foreign Affairs and Security. All parties in the coalition government of the day thus have a voice, at the cabinet level, in framing legislation on the armed forces; and at the Kneset level, while the larger opposition parties as a minority in the committees cannot in fact control the military budgets, they may at least get to know the contents. Informed Israelis sharply disagree on whether or not these constitute adequate civilian checks on the military establishment.[11]

The key to the puzzle is the Defense Minister, who serves, in effect, as the commander in chief of the armed forces, although his office does not expressly carry the title. Under the law, the Defense Minister need not consult with his cabinet colleagues or procure Kneset endorsement prior to taking major policy decisions, even such a one as mobilizing the reserve brigades. He must, it is true, bring such a mobilization order[12]

100

as soon as possible after it is issued . . . to the notice of the Knesset Committee on Security and Foreign Affairs [sic]. The Committee may confirm the order, with or without modifications, or refuse to confirm it, or place it before the Knesset. The order shall expire fourteen days after the date of its issue, except if, and as, confirmed by the Committee of Knesset prior to the termination of the said period.

In the event of a situation that seems to demand mobilization, however, is the Kneset likely to reverse the order of the Defense Minister?

The perennial Defense Minister, Ben Gurion, has towered above all other Israel politicians and has held the allegiance of a substantial part of the civilian population and of the military officers. Even among Ben Gurion's political enemies, respect for his judgment in a crisis has been widespread. The precedents that Ben Gurion has established in running the Defense Ministry and the armed forces have worked to limit institutional control over the military establishment. As a forceful leader, Ben Gurion has tended to make his decisions and then inform the cabinet, and sometimes the Kneset, too. Israel's constant state of siege has given him sufficient grounds for such freedom of action. Surrounded by hostile neighbors with populations far more numerous than its own, Israel has had no alternative to its policy of vigilance. Vacillation might be not only costly but fatal. One reason why Israel has managed to safeguard its security so well lies precisely in the steady, uncontested, and decisive leadership of the defense establishment.

Yet a lack of broader civilian controls does not mean, at least for the present, a lack of civilian supervision. Ben Gurion is a political leader, elected to office by popular franchise and subject to removal by popular will. The public outcry over the Lavon Affair illustrated the kind of political pressure that can be brought to bear on Ben Gurion to change his policies and to modify his manner. His refusal to do either produced a prolonged political deadlock in 1961. What is more, the precedents in bypassing checks and balances found in other democracies might conceivably complicate the future introduction of such checks and balances into Israel's governmental system.

In a symposium at Tel-Aviv, late in 1953, on Israel's army in the state and the society, S. N. Eisenstadt, one of the country's most gifted sociologists, suggested that the Prime Minister's invariable retention of the Defense Ministry represented a serious danger to Israel's democracy. Eisenstadt thought that such a combination, normal in a democracy

101

at war, was abnormal "in time of peace, and even in time of relative peace." [13] He felt that for one person to hold the two offices was to endow the army with the authority that attaches to the Prime Minister. Shortly after this symposium, the two offices were in fact separated in the first cabinet of Moshe Sharett, when Pinhas Lavon was named Minister of Defense and Sharett retained the Foreign Ministry.

This experiment, however, was hardly successful. The Lavon Affair is still somewhat obscure. It arose, however, from a dispute in the Defense Ministry, in the winter of 1954-55, over responsibility for an abortive act of sabotage in Cairo that was organized by Israel's military intelligence. Lavon sought to dismiss the director-general of the Defense Ministry (Shim'on Peres) and the chief of intelligence (Lieutenant Colonel Benjamin Gavli), who had issued the original order for the Cairo action. If the Prime Minister had supported his Defense Minister, he would have lost the ministry's chief of the General Staff Branch (Colonel Joseph Avidar) and other high-ranking officers. Sharett elected to support Peres and the army officers; Lavon resigned; and Ben Gurion returned to the Defense Ministry. The Lavon Affair scarcely provided conclusive evidence either for or against the separation of the Defense Ministry from the Prime Ministry "in times of relative peace." But it did underline a problem that apparently has never been adequately explored.

Any defense ministry with as many ramified activities as that of Israel must maintain almost constant liaison with all other major ministries: with Foreign Affairs, over the delicate problems posed by the ceaseless enmity of the Arab states and its repercussions among the great powers and the small; with Finance, over the progressively larger bites out of the government's annual appropriations that a swiftly modernizing military establishment must take; with Commerce and Industry, over questions of military imports, purchases, and sales; with Labor, over the most appropriate use of manpower; with Education and Culture, over the instructional program of the army and its premilitary training scheme; with Interior and Police, over the administration of the Arab areas; and with the Ministry of Agriculture, over the program of Nahal. It would seem that the Prime Minister is much better able than any other member of the cabinet to co-ordinate so many liaison efforts. The problem underlined by the Lavon Affair is likely to arise

102

again in the future if a division is made between the Prime Ministry and the Defense Ministry, unless the Prime Minister is designated commander in chief of the armed forces, so as to provide an institutional shield against the accidents of history.

The existing arrangement, however, poses a potential threat to Israel's security because of inadequate co-ordination of defense activities at the executive level. It also leaves unresolved the question of control over the framing of defense policy. It does not, however, endanger Israel's democracy. A citizen army, by definition, is the best assurance against that. The Permanent Service of Israel's ground forces, as has been seen, is a very small professional nucleus. These officers, commissioned and non-commissioned alike, do not even remotely constitute the principal repository of middle-class skills in the country; nor do they form a separate political group. Instead, they probably represent a cross-section of Israel's many parties. There thus appears very little danger of a military over-turn of the civilian regime in Israel.

Indeed, the shoe seems to be on the other foot. The danger is not one of military interference with politics, but of partisan political interference with the management of the defense establishment. In a multiple-party system with its sharp ideological differences on society, the economy, and the government, indecision is an ever present prospect, and it can affect security matters no less than others. Such indecision has been obviated, not by decisive leadership alone, but by Mapai's success in procuring a majority in every cabinet. The other parties may be dissatisfied with the way in which Ben Gurion and Mapai have been conducting the government; and the frequent changes in cabinet—the one formed in 1961 was the twelfth in less than fourteen years, and followed nine months of a care-taker regime—would confirm that the other parties in successive coalitions were not inhibited from expressing their lack of confidence in Mapai leadership. Nevertheless, with all the changes in government, security policy has preserved a remarkable degree of continuity.

Many academic and diplomatic observers have noted that the very presence of Israel in the Middle East has contributed much to the movement for Arab unity. Yet it might also be noted in reverse that the very minatory manner and attitude of the Arab states toward the unwanted neighbor in their midst serves as a potent unifying force in Israel, enabling the new state to make a virtue of its necessity. It has helped close the ranks of an ideologically divided country behind Ben Gurion's security policies.

When all is said and done, there is also the non-measurable contribution of personality. Perhaps the real durability of the system will be tested after the departure of the charismatic leader.

1. *Jerusalem Post*, November 24, 1961.

2. Ministery of Foreign Affairs, Department of Information, press release No. 1760, June 9, 1961.

3. Palmah is the abbreviation for *Plugot ha-Mahaz* or "Striking Units."

4. Text in *Sefer ha-Huqim 5709*, pp. 271-78; English translation in State of Israel, *Government Yearbook, 5711*, (1950), pp. 266-72.

5. Women may be exempted from service if they are mothers, pregnant, or married, or if they request exemption on grounds of conscience or religious conviction.

6. According to the amendment of August 26, 1952; under the original law of 1949, men served for twenty-four months and women for only twelve.

7. Don Peretz, *Israel and the Palestine Arabs* (Washington, D. C., 1959), chap. vi; see also *New York Times*, February 11, 1962.

8. Moshe Dayan, "Border Crossing Still Threat to Security," *Jerusalem Post*, September 29, 1961.

9. *The Citizen Army* (New York, 1957), pp. 169-70. Quoted by permission of St. Martin's Press, Inc. and Macmillan & Company, Ltd.

10. *Sinai Victory* (New York, 1958), p. 225.

11. See, for example, "Zava ve-Shilton Dimoqrati: Simpozion" ("Army and Democracy: A Symposium"), *Qeshet* (Spring, 1961), pp. 92-119.

12. Article 8 (b) of the Defense Service Law, from the text in State of Israel, *Government Yearbook, 5711*, p. 269.

13. Beit Hillel, *Ma'amado shel ha-Zava be-Israel: ba-Mdinah uva-Hevrah* (Tel-Aviv, 1954), p. 5.

The Role of the Military in the Middle East: Past Patterns and New Directions   JOHN C. CAMPBELL

ANY CONCLUSIONS, any judgments, on the intrusion of military officers into the politics of the Middle East must proceed from one salient and recognized fact: in that part of the world, force is a generally accepted means of political action. One need look no further in the historical record of the independent Middle Eastern states than those points that mark changes in government or regime to see the general pattern for the taking, holding, and transmission of political power. If there are no generally accepted rules of the game to keep the military out of politics, they are inevitably in it.

The only country with a consistent record of change through the democratic process of free elections is Israel; and even Israel's politics have had a somewhat special character with one political party, Mapai, in a dominant position ever since the founding of the state. Turkey had relatively free elections in the 1950's and, after the army's intervention in 1960, seems to be returning to them. But there the list stops. Constitutional democracy has not flourished elsewhere in the Middle East, where elections are generally "managed" by governments in power or where, as in the case of Lebanon, an agreed basis exists for sharing power among contending groups or factions, although even in Lebanon the compromise has been known to break down with consequent resort to force. In some countries the monarchy or ruling family appears to provide an element of stability and continuity; yet, if particular situations are examined, it is seen that the dynasties now ruling are hardly of long standing, most of them having come to power within the last generation by force or by the intervention of outside powers. The kings have already disappeared in Egypt and Iraq. Those who remain are not above politics but in it, and are, therefore, highly vulnerable to revolutionary change. Succession to a throne in the Middle East is rarely peaceful.

A monarchy, no less than a transient parliamentary regime, may be displaced overnight if it loses the support of its army. Who holds the political power has come to depend on who holds the military power. It is not surprising that the seizure or transferal of power by military coup d'état has become the normal procedure, especially in the Arab world.

The military in the Middle East, therefore, is generally the ultimate power, whether it is on the stage or in the background. It may be the basic continuing support for a king or a constitutional parliamentary regime. Or it may be a reserve power to be used only as a last resort; but, nevertheless, even when not used, it is always a potent influence of which political leaders and parties must take account. And increasingly there have been occasions when the army—or rather a group of officers in the army—comes out of the background to seize and exercise power. It may do so after defeat in war; or, because of a breakdown or discrediting of a civilian regime, it may move into what has become a political vacuum (as in Egypt in 1952 or Pakistan in 1958); or it may act against an unpopular regime that is trying to suppress all political opposition (as in Turkey in 1960). Often a group of officers may become convinced that they alone are called upon to act in behalf of the nation. They may consider themselves as holding a national mandate or embodying the national will. This was certainly the case in Egypt in 1952 and in Iraq in 1958. Such groups may have one or a number of aims, such as to restore values that have been lost or to implant new ones in the body politic, to assert national dignity, to throw out the foreigners, to end the old system of quarreling politicians and widespread corruption, or to speed modernization, economic devel-

106

opment, or social reform. Such aims create, or in any case they are used to justify, the will to power.

Thus an army gets into politics for a number of reasons. Perhaps the most compelling one is that in an unformed society the army is often the only institution that provides discipline, a sense of mission, education, and training in administrative and technical skills. Ambitious young men of other than the established ruling classes know that it is for them the route to political power. As military officers they see themselves as the new elite. And judging from the available evidence, a large part of the populace often seems to accept the advent of such men to power with few reservations, and sometimes with real enthusiasm. A lack of regret over the passing of a parliamentary system is, however, no proof of the popularity of military rule.

In the search for a set of rules or a pattern in the study of the role of the military beyond an appeal for further research into the historical experience of a dozen countries, the studies in this volume may provide a basis for some generalizations, and, above all, for a sorting out of trends and a definition of terms. It is true that the diversity of conditions—ranging from Lebanon to Libya, Israel to Iraq, Syria to Yemen—leads to the natural conclusion that there can be no general pattern. Still, in those states with roughly similar societies, the parallels exist, as Mr. Rustow's inquiry clearly shows. They justify looking, at least tentatively, across the board, and not merely country by country, to seek some general conclusions on the role of the military in Middle Eastern society, its accomplishments and failures, and its prospects for the future. Where the gaps and obscurities in the available knowledge of the subject counsel caution, it may still be worthwhile to point out questions for further exploration.

How do the general patterns, past and present, of the military's role in the society of other parts of the world apply to the contemporary Middle East? Perhaps some attempt at classification may be useful here. There are three situations that are relatively clear-cut and, one might say, extreme. One is that in which the army is a reflection of the society itself, such as the citizen army of Switzerland: the form of government is democratic and its control is civilian; the armed services merely represent the whole nation's participation in its own defense.

The second situation is precisely the opposite: the army is a force virtually outside the society but often interfering with or dominating it, a predatory force interested above all in gain and power for itself. This is a phenomenon that, in modern times, has appeared most starkly in some Latin American countries. The third situation is that of a purely professional, or mixed professional and conscript, military establishment wholly subordinate to the civilian government and sticking to its military tasks, such as those in Great Britain or the United States.

The remarkable thing about the Middle East is that so few of these extreme and clearly definable situations exist. Israel is the only example of a close identification of the military with society as a whole through universal military training and service. There is no example at all of the purely professional army under full civilian control. And although the armed forces in many Middle Eastern states from time to time have sought power and privilege at the expense of the people, there has not been, since the disappearance of the Turkish janissaries, a clear example of a predatory military force, undisciplined by political loyalties or institutions, exploiting a society for its own ends.

All other situations represent one form or another of the participation of the military in politics. In the Middle East, the historical record to date presents a picture of a continuing and sometimes overwhelming military presence in political life—especially in recent times, now that so many independent states with a woeful lack of experience in government are on the scene. This is a varied and changing picture with many gradations, but for purposes of exposition two general categories of political attitude and action can be distinguished.

The first category is that of an army that, along with other traditional elements of society—a monarchy, a landowning class, entrenched religion, as the case may be—acts in support of an established order. In such cases, the high-ranking officers in control of the armed forces are generally drawn from the ruling groups and serve the existing regime as a prop against those who would challenge or overthrow it. This has been the role of the army in Iran, where it has provided support for the Shah, and the Shah in turn has coddled the army by giving it positions of power and new equipment. Another example is Jordan, whose two kings, since the founding of the state, have depended on the traditional bedouin fighting forces as a counterweight to the

108

more modern and urban elements of the population acquired through the annexation of the west bank of the River Jordan and the influx of refugees from what is now Israel. Only the loyalty of those forces saved the throne in the crisis of April, 1957. In Saudi Arabia, the armed forces are mainly in the nature of tribal levies provided to the monarch by sheikhs and chiefs through a relationship based on fealty and regular subsidies.

The second general category, at the other end of the spectrum, is that of military as a force for revolution and reform. The path was set by Turkey, where young officers of the armed forces were in the forefront of the long struggle for modernization of the Ottoman Empire and then of the national movement for Turkish independence. They made possible the drastic reforms with which Kemal Atatürk brought Turkey into the world of the twentieth century. Now, in some of the Arab countries, much the same thing is transpiring. Generally, it is a movement of younger officers, many of them not from the upper classes, although some may be. The leaders are often of lower-middle-class origin. They are men vitally concerned with the backwardness of their society and desirous of changing it. Like the Young Turks and Kemal, they combine a zeal for reform with a new and more militant nationalism as they seek to build the strength and prestige of their countries. Their army careers and the arms at their disposal open the way to political action and the exercise of power. The new ideas may be largely those of intellectuals, but it is the military that brings them to the sphere of action. A vital question is whether there is, among their modernizing reforms, a provision for their own eventual retirement into the background, as was the case with the Kemalists in Turkey, so that civilian government will have a chance to work.

In the vanguard of the politically minded officers in the Arab world have been the groups often called "free officers," either secretly or openly organized, depending on the local political situation. These are the men who won power in Egypt and Iraq and have threatened to win it in other Arab countries. Gamal Abd al-Nasir is the striking example of at least apparent success. He and those who emulate him are, of course, interested in both the exercise of power and the special needs of the national military forces; but it is not power for its own sake that they desire. Nationalism is the basis of their political and ideological views. But modernization of society, instituting social reform, raising the living standards of the lower classes, and wiping out the privileges of the upper are also integral parts of their program. They have promised more than they have delivered. Yet "Arab socialism," vague as it is in content, is not merely a slogan or a façade but an idea with real meaning—a meaning that may change from one time to another, but an idea the basic direction of which remains unchanged.

In Egypt the army has held together. In Syria, over the years, it has tended to split into groups and factions. Many officers in the Syrian army have come from the ruling families, but the army still has had within its ranks a movement of younger officers interested in reform and political alliance with the more radical politicians, such as those of the Ba'th. The military absorption in the ups and downs of the game of politics before 1958, however, was so intense that no serious effort toward basic reform was made until Nasir, to his own misfortune, tried it. The military coup that broke Egypt's hold on Syria brought to the fore, temporarily at least, a relatively conservative-minded government, backed by an apparently united army. Yet one should not write off the potential of younger officers who, though they may have no taste for renewing the union with Egypt, should continue to represent a force for radical Arab nationalism and social change in Syria.

In Iraq the army has not asserted itself as a dominant force in the Qasim regime. Some of its officers have been associated with the nationalist elements, while others have, with Qasim, maintained a middle position among contending political factions. The Prime Minister seems to have become more and more of a lone leader, maneuvering between political factions and lacking a solid enough support in the armed forces to dominate the state with them alone. A new military elite has not yet emerged, but the revolution of 1958 sealed for good the fate of the monarchy and the old oligarchy, along with the conservative military men on which they relied. The political forces that come to the fore in the future are likely to find their origins or their support among the officers of the army who are in the middle ranks.

In other countries there are comparable stirrings in the armed forces, although officer groups strong enough to grasp the reins of power do not appear yet to have emerged. In Iran the younger and middle-rank army officers are the most likely source of any successful revolutionary change of regime. The possibility of there being a similar group in Turkey, where the army has re-established constitutional civilian government, should not be wholly discounted. The fourteen young officers who, during the period of government by the National Unity Committee, challenged the policy of General Gürsel that limited the army to the role of caretaker, represented a comparable desire for a dynamic military regime through which the younger officers could take some of the drastic measures they believed necessary to reform and modernize Turkish society.

What is of most interest, perhaps, is the actual performance of the military in power. In many countries their rule has been for a relatively brief span of time, but more and more evidence is coming in as the pattern of military rule becomes widely and solidly established. What is the actual record of the officers who have assumed unto themselves the mandate to rule in the name of the people?

Have they provided stable government? In Egypt, since 1954, one may say that they have. So also has Mohammed Ayub Khan's regime in Pakistan, although not quite fitting the "young officer" pattern. Iraq provides a contrast, in that General Qasim does not appear to represent a strong and cohesive group of army officers. Iraq is perhaps the least stable of any of the regimes established by military revolution. In Syria in past years, the military, whether Syria's or Egypt's, have shown no steady capacity to govern the country, but then neither has any other individual or group—Syria seems as close to being an ungovernable country as any in the world. Both the politicians and the military tend to have horizons stretching beyond the rather artificial frontiers of the Syrian republic.

Have the military cleaned out corruption? They have done so in part. Again Egypt and Pakistan are the best examples. The mere disappearance of the "old politicians," of course, does not automatically eliminate customs that have been deeply ingrained in a society for centuries. Yet there is little doubt that military rule has generally brought a greater honesty and discipline into public life, a housecleaning of sorts, a stricter and even Spartan sense of duty. In countries where corruption has been a way of life, it tends to creep back. Still, this is one aspect of politics on which the record of the military men has been relatively good and for which they should receive due credit.

Have the reformers in uniform really brought about a managed social revolution? Egypt's military regime started out with a land reform and on several occasions has taken measures of nationalization or expropriation against both foreigners and wealthy Egyptians. "Arab socialism," announced with much fanfare, promises a state-managed economy and a further leveling of income, though whether this will bring economic growth is another question. In Iraq the record of the Qasim regime is neither so long nor so indicative of basic reform. The revolution was made in the name of the people against the sheikhs and the old order, but neither in agrarian reform nor in general economic and social policy has the revolutionary government shown itself to be the architect of a new social order. Indeed, there is not even an adequate substitute for the development program of the old regime.

Yet, one thing seems certain: Where the young army officers of the new type have reached the seat of power, they have definitely broken with the past. Whether their record is one of success or of ineptitude and failure, there will be no return to the traditional order, not in Syria, nor Iraq nor Egypt. The conservative tinge apparent in the movement that took Syria out of the U.A.R. and in the first government of the once more independent Syrian republic did not represent the solid view of the army; and the military leaders remained in a position to move politicians in and out of office if and when they saw fit to do so.

For these very reasons, it is important for Western scholars to analyze what the military regimes are doing now: their progress in basic social reform, their constitutional innovations, their ability to build a more productive economy. Their successes or failures will have much to do with what comes next.

The signs all point to more, not less, military control of government in the states of the Middle East. As traditional regimes, with or without a façade of parliamentary institutions, reach the end of their allotted time, they seem most likely to be replaced by groups issuing from, or basing their strength on, the armed forces. Whether the new military regimes are the advance guard of democracy or of a new kind of authoritarian rule is far from clear. Nor, from the standpoint of the West, should it make so much difference, much as the spread of democratic institutions would be welcomed. The important task of the moment is to see how the military regimes develop, how they meet the demands and challenges of their own societies, and how well they succeed in guiding the process of change while strengthening their countries' independence.

The major problem facing Western policy in the Middle East is not the bases and military positions maintained there, nor the alliances that are signed and the doctrines that are proclaimed there: it is to find means of serving the common interests that exist among the Middle Eastern nations so that they can be helped to achieve their independence and realize their aspirations in ways that do not imperil the aims of the West. There need be no fundamental clash of destinies between the West and the Middle East. The problem is to get over the immensely difficult period of transition that has been marked by a virulently anti-Western nationalism (especially among the Arabs), an unsolved and apparently insoluble Palestine dispute, and a situation where the lure of Soviet arms and the gains of playing East and West against each other are so very tempting to Middle Eastern leaders. The West must get through this period of inevitable tension in its relations with the Middle East, while laying the basis for a future stage of mutual tolerance and co-operation.

The tasks ahead demand, on the part of Western governments and peoples, a real understanding of what is happening in the society and politics of the Middle East, especially in relation to the role of the military. Western diplomacy must know how best to influence the trend of developments through military and economic-aid programs and other contacts. This is no prescription for a new imperialism. The decisions on the future of the Middle East will rest with the peoples of the Middle East. But the West must use its influence to find that common ground on which the future relations with the Middle Eastern nations can properly and safely rest. Yet the West cannot act unless it understands the political equations, the motive forces that will provide the direction for Middle Eastern developments.

In gaining that understanding, the resources of government are naturally of the greatest importance in the essential tasks of reporting from the field and analyzing all current intelligence. Scholarly inquiry must play its part also, particularly in coping with the long-range questions that appear as one looks backward into history and forward into the future. This is not an argument that scholarship's only role is to aid in the formation of government policy. The scholars themselves would be the first to protest such a conclusion. The search for truth has its own justification. Nevertheless, so long as scholars work in the contemporary field, there is, and should be, an intimate connection between scholarship and public policy.

On this subject of the role of the military in the Middle East, the contributors to this volume have performed a real service in opening up questions that require a continuing search for data, for explanations, and for periodic analysis of the requirements of policy. Without the interpretation and judgment on which an understanding of the role of the military can be based, the future prospects for good and fruitful relations with the Middle East will be dim indeed.

Appendix

Training for Leadership in World Affairs
WILLIAM R. POLK

IT IS a great honor to participate in the opening of the new Graduate Institute for World Affairs at the Ohio State University. To improve upon the statement of purpose contained in the formal announcement of the Institute is difficult.

> Today, in a rapidly evolving and expanding international life, an effective knowledge of the contents, methods, and formulated concepts of the many fields of study concerned with World Affairs is imperative. . . . Scholars must take cognizance of these developments in order to understand more fully world society as it exists; policy makers in every sphere of human activity must reckon with diverse powers at their command; and teachers, business executives, civilian and military government officials, and public opinion molders must be trained to have a fuller understanding of the dynamics involved in the integration advancing in every direction. In this age, World Affairs know no boundaries and permeate every academic discipline.

These thoughts are of great importance, for the links between government and universities are two-way streets. There is, and should be, constant interchange of ideas, peoples, and materials between the two. And at the same time, to be effective the two should be conscious of their different roles, their limitations, and their attributes.

117

In the first year of the Kennedy administration, a great deal of notice was given to the infusion of academic people into government. It is important, however, to recognize that this movement is constant. A number of people went to Washington from various universities every year under the previous administration. And, equally important, under this and previous administrations, many have left government and joined the universities. Of the last four chairmen of the Policy Planning Council of the Department of State, one has come from business, one from the law, and two from academic life, and one upon retiring from the chairmanship went into academic life. There are now countless academicians and government officials who have served in both government and the universities.

The dichotomy between the universities and government is not in personnel; rather it exists in differences in function and point of view. Government is constantly involved in a stream of decisions. Those of yesterday influence the ones of tomorrow in a continuous chain that is almost impossible to break or interrupt. Positions are taken that commit the takers to a direction of action. In a sense, decisions have a tendency ultimately to make themselves.

In the universities, to the contrary, there is a useful distance from immediate responsibility. This is not to say that the people in universities are not involved and responsible in world affairs. They are, of course, often passionately and deeply involved. They may have superior knowledge and a wider perspective than those directly and immediately concerned in government. But what is much more important, people outside of government do not have to make immediate decisions; they did not make yesterday's, and so they are free to consider and reconsider those of tomorrow to a degree that is often not possible for people on the front line. This freedom can be a source of vigor, of useful criticism, and of needed advice to those who are caught up in the daily stream of events.

On its side, government has a major asset that is, to the academicians, most impressive. To have at one's disposal the vast resources of the Department of State is an exhilarating experience. There is a wealth of knowledge available to people in government like nothing most academicians have ever seen in outside research organizations, universities, or learned societies.

118

Yet, as able as it is in gathering information, the government must always be the weaker in its ability to generate fresh points of view on given problems. It has lived with many problems too long. Because of the very complexity of governmental structure, it is often easier and more expeditious to handle such complicated topics as the role of the military in emerging societies in an academic atmosphere. Moreover, as the authors of these papers vividly illustrate, the available expertise on any given topic is spread throughout government, universities, and the business community; and the constructive role of universities in assembling talent and in directing it to major, but not immediate, problems and opportunities is a most valuable one. All too often those who are very close to day-to-day, week-to-week, problems in conducting foreign relations find it difficult to pull back and take the longer view that is so necessary for the success of short-term programs and actions.

But above all, government is in constant need of fresh blood, of new people coming to to carry on its vital functions, for never before in the history of the United States has there been a greater complexity in international relations.

It is amazing to look around Washington and to find the tremendous number of organizations involved in making decisions, many of them far-reaching and of importance for many years ahead in numerous fields of foreign activity. There is, of course, the United States Information Agency (USIA), which is responsible for numerous broadcasting and publication programs in many languages and in many parts of the world, and which has overseas facilities that generate extremely intricate problems of staffing and organization. The Commerce Department has a very vigorous and growing international section. The Agriculture Department, the Treasury, and the Pentagon, of course, all have important international sections. Even the Department of the Interior, through its Office of Saline Water, is empowered to operate abroad. Our embassies reflect the wide diversity of these overseas relations. Almost any embassy is filled with attachés from numerous governmental departments.

In looking back from today's complexity, diplomacy in the early years of the nineteenth century has a fairy-tale atmosphere. One might say, "Once upon a time many, many years ago, foreign affairs demanded a little knowledge of diplomacy, some passing information on com-

119

merce, and an amateur interest in military strategy." Today, this is very far from reality; specialized knowledge is required in virtually the entire range of human endeavor. In the Department of State, the Bureau of Educational and Cultural Affairs, for example, is concerned with everything from the Harlem Globe Trotters and King Tut's treasures to book production in many languages and student missions to international conferences. The Office of the Science Adviser is a clearing house for information on policy matters related to science, and advises UN agencies, United States government agencies, industry, universities, and other segments of society. The External Research Division and the Historical Office maintain ties with American research organizations and universities. Intelligence and Research, a vigorous part of the Department of State, gathers vast amounts of factual data on events all over the world. And the new Agency for International Development (AID) deals with developmental problems in a vast part of the world's area.

To illustrate the diversity as well as the intricacy of governmental operations and policy determination, it is appropriate here to discuss the Policy Planning Council of the Department of State, and, in particular, since the Middle East is the area under consideration at this conference, to relate its duty and work in assisting in the formulation of American policy toward the countries of the Middle East.

The Middle East is an area in which many branches of the United States government have interests; many even have separate programs there. But primary responsibility rests upon the Department of State's Bureau of Near Eastern and South Asian Affairs. The Policy Planning Council works closely with this bureau and helps to determine what are reasonable goals, to set some priorities in their achievement, and to select appropriate means of action. Being one step removed from day-to-day actions and not responsible for yesterday's deeds, the Council tries to take a somewhat longer and more detached look than can those more directly involved.

"Policy-planning" is not a mysterious or enigmatic term; it is just another name for a thought process that most individuals go through in their daily lives. Sometimes one does it explicitly but just as often, implicitly. The young man who chooses a career, a college, or a job; the doctor who prescribes a medicine; the lawyer who determines whether or not to take legal action in a suit; the housewife who decides on a menu—all go through a thought process that can be fairly and simply described as "policy-planning." When faced with a problem, one must identify the reality of the situation as well as one can, decide what is desired and what can reasonably be achieved, and then choose the best means of action. Furthermore, because one realizes the limitations of his abilities and the changing nature of the world, he also prepares for "contingencies," those unlikely situations that occasionally arise to cause the best-laid plans of mice and men to go astray. Often success in life is directly proportional to the care taken in each of these steps. If a romantic or unrealistic view of a situation is taken, the resulting actions will not be well directed; if goals are set too high, each achievement, no matter how real, can only be a "failure"; and if no preparation is made for "contingencies," one may be caught short or miss unusual opportunities.

Policy-planning can be fairly simple or extraordinarily complex. In business, an executive may have an elaborate study made of several market potentialities, plant efficiency, or product diversification. The housewife, in preparing a soufflé, may keep a TV dinner in the freezer. Anyone, before setting out on a long drive, even if he has not planned a definite itinerary or fixed a destination, does make sure of a spare tire in the car. In short, the process is very familiar and its difficulty depends upon the task at hand; in most daily chores it is so simple that one does not identify it as a way of thought. But in something as far ranging as the foreign policy of a great power, covering a vast area of a world that is changing at a revolutionary pace, and about which knowledge is always imperfect, policy-planning is an immense task.

How might the policy planner look at the Middle East, the area under discussion at this conference? The first question he would face would be how important is the area, who is interested in it, and why is the United States concerned? In response, he would discover that the Middle East is important to the United States for several reasons. First, it is situated on the air, sea, and land routes that link Europe, Asia, and Africa. Throughout history, the Middle East has been the world's highway. Even in those times when its political states have been weak, they have commanded international attention. Today, with increased dependence upon communications, transportation, and travel,

121

the Middle East plays a crucial role in the lives and hopes of the entire world.

Secondly, the vast oil resources of the Middle East provide the power that turns the wheels of Europe. Control of Middle Eastern oil was an avowed goal of the armies of World War I and II. At present, Europe can be supplied from other sources—North Africa, South America, and the United States—but at greater cost. In assessing the importance of this flow of oil, it is well to remember what while Europe *can* get oil elsewhere, the Middle East has not yet been able to sell oil, in the vast quantities now produced, elsewhere.

Thirdly, as the birthplace of three great world religions, Judaism, Christianity, and Islam, as a leader in the Afro-Asian bloc of non-aligned powers, and as a center of educational institutions having a significant impact beyond the region itself, the Middle East plays an important role in American policy considerations in other quarters of the globe. Since Russia has traditionally aspired for hegemony in the Middle East, negotiated with the Nazis for recognition of these dreams, and pursued an active policy there in recent years, the United States must exercise a special vigilance to help nations of that area to preserve their independence and freedom.

And fourthly, the Middle Eastern countries are today experiencing a major social revolution. Old ways of life are giving way to new; old expectations have been shelved for much higher goals; new political arrangements are being sought. In this political and social kaleidoscope, ample opportunities exist for crises, wars, and frustrations as dangerous for Americans as they are harmful to the people of the Middle East.

In this context, the United States is herself a "third force." America plays this role in three separate ways. While it is recognized that the quarrels between the Arab states and Israel must be settled by their own efforts, the United States seeks to mitigate the worst aspects of hostility as well as to search for ways in which the region can find a just and lasting peace. The states wish to retain their independence and to evolve that pattern of life most suited to their cultural heritage and aspirations. But the Soviet Union works to impose upon them a political ideology—communism—and to incorporate them into her

122

vast empire. The United States stands to assist the Middle Eastern states in maintaining their independence.

Even without these two dangers to the peace and prosperity of the Middle East, the disparity between the reality in which people live and the goals that they have accepted—what has been vividly called the "frustration gap"—can only be reconciled by constructive action in mobilizing and improving local resources, both human and physical. In this task, the United States has provided and will continue to provide major assistance. It will be noted that the United States does not wish for herself any special privileges or advantages; and yet, for many reasons, the Middle East is vitally important to the United States in securing the sort of world in which all can live.

The next question before the policy planner is what is the "effective reality" he faces. What are those facts of geography, history, culture, economics, politics, aspirations, and social organization that define the character of Middle Eastern peoples and those with whom they deal? One can never completely know this, of course, because the subjects are human; if he could, the policy planner could do his work once and then go home. But the planner must constantly try to gain more precise knowledge so as to make better decisions and plans.

In a very broad generalization, the Middle East is a huge, mostly barren, arid region, containing only one major mineral resource, oil, lacking a potential for industrialization on a major scale, and having a population internally divided and weakened by disease, poverty, and illiteracy. Also it is the scene of an accelerating social revolution, an upheaval partly of Western making. Schools, books, movies, and many Western examples foster the notion that a better way of life is possible. Industry and commerce alter the ways in which people make their living, and aid programs create some of the muscle of modernization. On many things the people are divided, but there is a consensus that the present, with its evidence of backwardness, must give way to a brighter future. Just what this brighter future is to be, how one is to achieve it, and who is to benefit most from it are points on which there is as yet no general agreement. For outsiders, the key element appears to be the accent on change.

123

Underlying much of the social and political confusion of the Middle East is the bitter conflict between the Arabs and Israel. The former, from the vantage points of their consciousness of present weakness, memories of a proud past, and desires for a richer future, view Israel as a new sort of intrusion from the West, an impediment to Arab unity, a threat to their security, and a symbol of their failure. To the Arabs, therefore, the Palestine problem acquires a transcendence over those world problems which people in the United States regard as vital.

Both the United States and the Soviet Union voted for the 1947 United Nations Partition Resolution. Since that time, the United States has continued to help Israel with large-scale governmental and private contributions, but occasionally has also opposed Israeli moves and has supported United Nations motions to censure Israel for aggressions. The United States has also assisted on a large scale in developmental projects of the Arabs and has paid a major share of the bills for keeping the Arab refugees alive. Essentially, the United States secured the withdrawal of France, Great Britain, and Israel from Egypt after their attack on Suez. The U.S.S.R., however, has completely reversed her 1947 position and has endeavored, by capitalizing on the Palestine dispute and Arab fears of the West, to secure positions of advantage among the Arabs. Unlike the United States, the Soviet Union manages to avoid responsibility for her part in the creation of Israel and has not helped to support the Palestine refugees.

Israel has received in the years since her formation far more outside assistance per capita than the Arab states and has used these gifts and loans with vigor and wisdom. As a result, Israel is today on the way to becoming a modern Western state with a per capita gross national product eleven times that of Jordan and three times that of her nearest Middle Eastern rival, Lebanon. The Arabs recognize this economic superiority and fear it.

In the face of what they regard as the threat of Israel and in recognition of their own serious internal disunity—the cultural gap between the sophisticated man of Beirut and the bedouin of the desert, the religious split between the various minorities, and the political rivalry between states and rulers—in the face of these serious divisions, the Arabs have attempted to create mechanisms and an ideology to bring

124

about unity. In spite of failures up to now, the presuppositions upon which these unifying attempts have been based remain popular, and future attempts at unification can be anticipated.

The Middle East is also the scene of rivalry between the Soviet Bloc and the Western powers. From a stance of neutrality the Arabs have anticipated not only obtaining military and economic assistance from both sides but also preventing either side from achieving a dominant position within the Middle East. The Soviet Union has been willing to give aid on the ideological justification that at this stage of development the "bourgeois" regimes of the Middle East are "progressive" by comparison with the regimes they replace, and on the political calculation that the problems the Middle Eastern governments face in the midst of a revolutionary situation are so serious as ultimately to destroy them. In these circumstances, the Soviet planner might reason Soviet aims will be accomplished at minimum cost to the U.S.S.R. and maximum cost to the United States.

The United States, not desiring to dominate or subvert the region or to force an ideology upon the people living there, acts with less unity of purpose than the Soviet Union but also acts in ways which ultimately, it is hoped, will be recognized by the Middle East as more acceptable than those of the Soviet Union. It should be stressed, moreover, that even should the United States wish, she could not realistically hope to reverse the neutralism of the Arab countries except at prices she would not consent to pay. In outline, this is the "effective reality" with which the policy planner must deal.

In these circumstances, what are reasonable American goals—not "pie in the sky," which could not be eaten even if reached, but those objectives that, given America's other commitments, her approach to international politics, and the present world, can be realistically expected? National as well as personal goals may be set so high that one always fails to reach them, no matter how brilliant the attempt. Lack of realism—the setting of impossible tasks—is as much a mistake in international relations as in personal life.

American goals in the Middle East are few in number and may be stated simply. America wants the countries of the area to retain their independence. She seeks to prevent hostilities that might lead to war. The United States wants a sufficient flow of oil to meet the requirements

125

of world industry. She wishes for herself and her friends rights of peaceful passage and intercourse. These might be said to be primary goals. Other American policy goals are the evolution of strong, popular governments able and willing to meet the challenges of the future; the growth of more friendly relations among all Middle Eastern states and the United States; and, most earnestly, progress toward a peaceful solution of the Palestine problem.

These goals do not seem unrealistic nor are they less than the demands that security requires. But no one reaches his goals just by understanding what the world is like and by stating his goals. He must establish lines of action appropriate to the task and within the limits of his resources and other commitments.

Perhaps the major line of action the United States follows may be seen in the pronouncements by her representatives that the government intends to act to preserve her interests and to support those governments that are striving to uphold their independence against aggression or subversion. In numerous, much less publicized ways, American policy is made known daily over the radio, in the press, and through representatives in the capitals of the world. Similarly, through receptivity to requests and the search for opportunities, the United States makes clear to the governments and peoples of the Middle East that they can look to her for support and example in building the strength and capability necessary for improving their way of life and retaining their independence.

When American help is offered, an attempt is made to assure all concerned that Americans not only demand independence for themselves but firmly and clearly respect it in others. American society is pluralistic: there is no one creed, no dogma, no ideology by which it allows itself to be judged or by which it judges others. In view of the different heritages of the world's peoples, it is realized that the American way of life is not necessarily suited to people in every part of the world. So America seeks and hopes others will seek "life, liberty, and the pursuit of happiness." To that goal, there are several roads and Americans are able to understand those traveling different roads.

To many in the Middle East, the Soviet Union is an unknown quality; communism is untried. It seems to offer those shortcuts, those quick, black-and-white solutions that men follow when they are bewildered and desperate. So, while the United States offers help to the Middle Easterners in finding their own ways to meet the challanges of the present and to rise to the needs of the future, she seeks also to demonstrate the incompatibility of communism and the aspirations of the Middle East and to expose the power politics of the Soviet Union and the communist Chinese.

These are no idle propaganda gambits; the Russians and Chinese, by their actions in the Balkans and in Asia, by their attacks upon nationalism, and by the models they demonstrate of their utopias, themselves do much to disillusion the people in the Middle East.

In a way reminiscent of American isolationists, however, many in the Middle East find Hungary and Viet Nam far away and of little significance. Every effort is made, therefore, to explain the relevance of the American belief in "One Law," one standard of conduct for all the world.

This is most difficult, of course, when America comes to deal with those issues of the Middle East about which passions are most intense: in the Palestine dispute, the United States tries to convince both Arabs and Israelis of her impartiality. Both are informed that America stands behind United Nations efforts to bring peace and that she will support strict observance of the armistice agreement. She has supported and continues to support the United Nations Relief and Works Agency with food and money to care for Arab refugees.

Recognizing that men must have tangible evidence of improvement in order to work constructively for the future, the United States provides those states that wish her help with technical and financial assistance in their programs for development. Through tax incentives and, where possible or useful, through guarantees, American business is encouraged to put its capital and skill usefully to work abroad. In addition to sending out technical and managerial people, America is working to develop a Middle Eastern capacity for self-improvement by bringing students, officials, businessmen, journalists, and army officers to the United States for tours or study. Many of these come as guests of the government; others as guests of foundations and universities. Where the problem is hunger, other governments are assisted through the Food for Peace Program in better meeting the needs of their peoples.

127

Realizing that money spent on weapons cannot be used productively to create that atmosphere of security and hope in the future for which so many strive, the United States urges her friends not to weaken themselves over the longer term in order to gain apparent strength in the present. But where this is not possible, America tries to hold a sufficient balance of arms to prevent recourse to war.

These, in very broad outline, are the categories into which fall the thousands of separate actions taken by all departments of the government and hundreds of American universities, foundations, and businesses in any year.

Lastly, the policy planner attempts to foresee those "contingencies," the unexpected "flat tires," which interrupt the progress of the people of the Middle East and the United States toward a better life, toward peace and security. Contingencies are inevitable in a world of change; the planner seeks, therefore, to identify likely contingencies and to take steps to be ready for them or to be able to take such acts in advance so as to avoid the most dangerous aspects they present. Planning, thought, constant reassessment of knowledge, consultations with friends, daily intercourse with the peoples of the entire world rarely appear—or can appear—on the surface. Newcomers to government never fail to be amazed at the amount of effort that thousands of dedicated men and women in Washington, and all over the world, devote to this task. By its very nature, this is a job never well enough done, never finished; it is a job as complex as any the world can present. It cannot be simplified, and those who believe that there are shortcuts to easy answers reveal a dangerous misunderstanding of the world.

Foreign policy planning demands all of the skill, understanding, patience, and knowledge that government, universities, and business can command. There must be people trained to cope with a multiplicity of specialized information in the many fields pertinent to any given problem. As these problems grow more complex in the years ahead— and they will—American society will have to produce more trained people.

Few tasks in our society can have a higher priority in the years ahead, and such a development as the Graduate Institute for World Affairs at the Ohio State University can and will make a great contribution to the national purpose.

128

Notes on the Contributors

JOHN C. CAMPBELL, director of political studies for the Council on Foreign Relations, is the author of *Defense of the Middle East*. For many years he was an officer of the Department of State and served for some time as a member of the Policy Planning Council.

SYDNEY NETTLETON FISHER, professor of history and co-ordinator of the Graduate Institute for World Affairs at the Ohio State University, is the author of *The Middle East: A History* and *The Foreign Relations of Turkey, 1481-1512*. He edited *Social Forces in the Middle East* and served as editor of the *Middle East Journal*.

J. C. HUREWITZ, professor of government, the Graduate Faculty of Political Science of Columbia University, is the author of *The Struggle for Palestine; Middle East Dilemmas;* and *Diplomacy in the Near and Middle East*.

MAJID KHADDURI, professor in, and director of, the Center for Middle East Studies at the School of Advanced International Studies of The Johns Hopkins University, is the author of *Independent Iraq; War and Peace in the Law of Islam; Islamic Jurisprudence;* etc.

129

GEORGE KIRK, lecturer on government and on the modern history of the Middle East at Harvard University, is the author of *A Short History of the Middle East; The Middle East in the War, 1939-1945; The Middle East, 1945-1950;* and *Contemporary Arab Politics.*

WILLIAM R. POLK, member of the Policy Planning Council of the Department of State and former professor of history at Harvard University, has studied and traveled extensively in the Middle East. He is the author of a forthcoming book on the social and economic developments in Lebanon and Syria from 1780 to 1840.

DANKWART A. RUSTOW, professor of international social forces at Columbia University and senior research analyst for The Brookings Institution, is the author of *The Politics of Compromise* and *Politics and Westernization in the Near East;* and co-author of *Islam and the West* and *The Politics of the Developing Areas.*

GORDON H. TORREY, consultant to the United States government on Middle Eastern political matters, has resided and studied in Syria and Lebanon, and is the author of a forthcoming book on the political and military interrelationships in Syria from 1945 to 1958.

Index

131

132

Hottinger, Arnold, 87
Hourani, George, 84
Hulagu, Mongol Khan, 5
al-Hunaydi, Captain Ahmad, of Syria, 63, 68
Hungary, 6, 127
Huntington, Samuel P., 19
Hurewitz, J. C., 89-104, 129
Husayn, King of Jordan, 4, 108

Ikha party, Iraq, 12
In the Country of the White Lilies, see Beyaz Zambaklar Memleketinde
Ince Memed, 33
India, 10
Inönü, President and General Ismet, 4, 21-22, 24, 26, 35, 37-38
International Bank for Reconstruction and Development, 77
International Press Institute, May 30, 1961, 92
Iran, 3, 8, 12, 16, 20
    army in, 108, 110
    military training, 16
Iraq, 6, 8, 10, 15-16, 18-20, 41-51, 53, 55, 58, 61-62, 65, 106-7, 129
    coup of 1934, 41
    coup of 1936, 41
    coups of 1936-41, 13
    coup of 1938, 13, 41
    coup of 1940-41, 41-42
    coup of 1948, 41-44
    coup of 1952, 41, 43-44
    coup of 1956, 41, 43
    democratic ideas in, 42
    Free Officers, 44-45, 109
    independence, 41
    military dictatorships, 50
    military training, 16
    Muslims, 50
    Revolution of 1958, 3, 11, 13, 15, 41-42, 44-47, 106, 110
Irgun Zvai Leumi (National Military Organization), Israel, 95
Islam, 5-6, 47-49, 76, 122
Isma'il, Khedive of Egypt, 7, 72
Isma'ilya, Battle of, 75
Ismet, *see* Inönü

Israel, 4, 8-10, 16, 18, 57, 60, 65, 74-75, 89-104, 107-9, 122, 124, 127
    Arab policy, 93
    citizen army, 95
    Civil Defense (Hitgonenut Ezrahit), 96
    Committee on Foreign Affairs and Security, 90-91, 100-102, 104
    Defense Ministry, 89-91, 97-98, 100-103
    Defense Service Law, 95-96
    General Staff, 91
    Military Security Committee, 91
    military training, 16
    Ministerial Security Committee, 91
    navy, 97
    security problems, 92
Israel-Arab war of 1948, 91
Israeli-Syrian Mixed Armistice Commission, 61
Istanbul, 10, 27-31, 45
Istanbul, University of, 24
Italy, Italians, 28
Italian Criminal Code, 27
Italian War with Turkey, 24
Izmir, 28

Janissary Corps, 6
Jargy, Simon, 87
Jaurès, 33
Jews, 73
Jinnah, Muhammad, 56
Johnson, John J., 20
Jordan, 3, 16, 20, 45, 62, 75, 92, 124
    crisis of April, 1957, 109
    military training, 16
Jordan, River, 109
Judaism, 122
Justice party, Turkey, 21, 36-38

Kamil Pasha, Grand Vezir, 10-11
Karabekir, Kâzim, 7
Karaman, Lieutenant Colonel S., 30, 39
Kemal, Mustafa, *see* Atatürk
Kemal, Yaşar, 33, 39-40
Kerekes, Tibor, 87

134

135